Abby Maria Hemenway

Songs of the War

Abby Maria Hemenway

Songs of the War

ISBN/EAN: 9783337516505

Printed in Europe, USA, Canada, Australia, Japan

Cover: Foto ©Thomas Meinert / pixelio.de

More available books at **www.hansebooks.com**

PART I.

Songs of the War.

"THE UNION OF LAKES, THE UNION OF LANDS,
THE UNION OF STATES NONE CAN SEVER;
THE UNION OF HEARTS, THE UNION OF HANDS,
AND THE FLAG OF OUR UNION FOREVER."

ALBANY:
J. MUNSELL, 78 STATE STREET.
1863.

202. —— Songs of the War. (By J. H. Boker, Bayard Taylor,
G. W. Bungay, Robert Lowell, Bryant, Aldrich, Holmes, Newell,
Longfellow and others.) 12mo, stiff wrappers.

Songs of the War.

"THE UNION OF LAKES, THE UNION OF LANDS,
THE UNION OF STATES NONE CAN SEVER;
THE UNION OF HEARTS, THE UNION OF HANDS,
AND THE FLAG OF OUR UNION FOREVER."

ALBANY:

J. MUNSELL, 78 STATE STREET.

1863.

SONGS OF THE WAR.

AD POETAS.

BY GEORGE H. BOKER.

O brother bards, why stand ye silent all,
    Amidst these days of noble strife,
While drum and fife, and the fierce trumpet-call,
    Awake the land to life.

Now is the time, if ever time there was,
    To strike aloud the sounding lyre,
To touch the heroes of our holy cause
    Heart-deep with ancient fire.

'Tis not for all, like Norman Taillefere,
    To sing before the warlike horde
Our fathers' glories, the great trust we bear,
    And strike with harp and sword.

Nor yet to frame a lay whose moving rhyme
    Shall flow in music North and South,
And fill with passion, till the end of time,
    The nations' choral mouth.

Yet surely, while our country rocks and reels,
    Your sweetly-warbled olden strains
Would mitigate the deadly shock she feels,
    And soothe her in her pains.

Some knight of old romance, in full career,
    Heard o'er his head the sky-lark sing,
And pausing, leaned upon his bloody spear,
    Lost in that simple thing.

If by your songs no heroes shall be made
　　To look death boldly eye to eye,
They may glide gently to the martyr's aid
　　When he lies down to die.

And many a soldier, on his gory bed,
　　May turn himself, with lessened pain,
And bless you for the tender words you said,
　　Now singing in his brain.

So ye, who hold your breath amidst the fight,
　　Be to your sacred calling true ;
Sing on ! the far result is not in sight
　　Of the great good ye do.

SUMTER—April 12-15, 1861.

BY GEORGE W. BUNGAY.

[From *The Call for Volunteers.*]

The iron drops on Sumter fall.

Shall our good swords in scabbards rust,
Our flag dishonored, trail in dust,
　　When rebels seek our subjugation ?
Perish the thought ! Our blades are drawn,
Thick as the summer blades of corn,
　　Swift to defend our bleeding nation.

The breach in Sumter's battered walls,
With black lips to the nation calls,
　　To rise, from inland to the borders.
Our flag of stars, by' traitors' slaves
Trod in the dust, in triumph waves,
　　With stripes for cowards and marauders.

Oh, clang the old bell in the tower,
That spoke for freedom in the hour
　　" That tried the souls " of bravest mortals.
Let patriots rock old Faneuil Hall,
And mantles on our heroes fall,　　　　　[als.
　　From those who climbed Fame's starry port-
　　　　　　　　　　　　　—*N. Y. Tribune.*

THE GATHERING.

Forward ! onward ! far and forth !
An earthquake shout awakes the North.
　　　Forward !

Massachusetts hears that cry—
Hears, and gives the swift reply,
　　　Forward !

Pennsylvania draws her sword,
Echoes from her hills the word,
　　　Forward !

Brave New York is up and ready,
With her thirty thousand steady,—
　　　Forward !

Small Rhode Island flies to arms,
Shouting at the first alarms,
　　　Forward !

Illinois and Indiana
Shriek, as they unroll our banner,
　　　Forward !

Not behind the rest in zeal,
Hear Ohio's thunder-peal,
　　　Forward !

From Vermont, New Hampshire, Maine,
Comes the same awakening strain,
　　　Forward !

Old Connecticut is here,
Ready to give back the cheer,
　　　Forward !

Minnesota, though remote,
Swells the free, inspiring note,
　　　Forward !

Iowa and Michigan,
Both are ready to a man—
　　　Forward !

Not the last in honor's race,
See Wisconsin come apace—
            Forward !

Delaware, New Jersey, rise
And put on.their martial guise,
            Forward !

Onward ! On ! a common cause
Is yours—your liberties and laws.
            Forward !

Forward, in your strength and pride !
God himself is on your side.
            Forward !
                                —*Boston Transcript.*

WAR SONNET.

BY WILLIAM H. BURLEIGH.

Thank God ! the free North is awake at last !
    When burning cannon shot and bursting shell,
    Was from the red mouth of yon Vulcan's hell,
Rained on devoted Sumpter thick and fast ;
The sleep of ages from her eyelids past,
    One bound—and lo ! she stands erect and tall,
    While Freedom's host come trooping to her call,
Like eager warriors to the trumpet's blast !
Woe to the traitors and their robber horde,
    Woe to the spoilers who pollute the land,
    When a roused nation terrible and grand,
Grasps in a holy cause the avenging sword,
And swears, from Treason's bloody clutch to save
The priceless heritage our fathers gave.
                                —*N. Y. Tribune.*

THE MASSACHUSETTS LINE.

BY ROBERT LOWELL.

Air—*Yankee Doodle.*

Still first, as long and long ago,
    Let Massachusetts muster;
Give her the post right next the foe;
    Be sure that you may trust her.
She was the first to give her blood
    For freedom and for honor;
She trod her soil to crimson mud:
    God's blessing be upon her.

She never faltered for the right,
    Nor ever will hereafter;
Fling up her name with all your might,
    Shake roof-tree and shake rafter.
But of old deeds she need not brag,
    How she broke sword and fetter;
Fling out again the old strip'd flag!
    She'll do yet more and better.

In peace her sails fleck all the seas,
    Her mills shake every river;
And where are scenes so fair as these
    God and her true hands give her?
Her claim in war who seeks to rob?
    All others come in later—
Hers first it is to front the Mob,
    The Tyrant and the Traitor.

God bless, God bless the glorious State!
    Let her have way to battle!
She'll go where batteries crash with fate,
    Or where thick rifles rattle.
Give her the Right, and let her try,
    And then, who can, may press her;
She'll go straight on, or she will die;
    God bless her! and God bless her!

Duanesburgh, May 7, 1861.   —*N. Y. Evening Post.*

IN BALTIMORE.

BY BAYARD TAYLOR.

Oh, city of our country's song,
      By that swift aid we bore,
When sorely pressed, receive the throng,
Who go to shield our flag from wrong,
And give us welcome warm and strong,
      In Baltimore!

We had no arms, as friends we came,
      As brothers evermore,
To rally round one sacred name,
The charter of our power and fame;
We never dreamed of guilt and shame
      In Baltimore.

The coward mob upon us fell;
      McHenry's flag they tore;
Surprised, borne backward by the swell,
Bent down with mad inhuman yell,
Before us yawned a traitorous hell
      In Baltimore !

The streets our soldiers' fathers trod,
      Blushed with their children's gore;
We saw the craven rulers nod,
And dip in blood the civic rod—
Shall such things be, O righteous God,
      In Baltimore?

No, never! By that outrage black,
      A solemn oath we swore,
To bring the Keystone's thousands back;
Strike down the dastards who attack,
And leave a red and fiery track
      Through Baltimore!

Bow down in haste thy guilty head !
      God's wraft is swift and sore;
The sky with gathering bolts is red—

Cleanse from thy skirts the slaughter shed,
Or make thyself an ashen bed—
    Oh Baltimore!

———

SEND THEM HOME TENDERLY.

"I pray you to cause the bodies of the Massachusetts soldiers dead in Baltimore, to be immediately laid out, and tenderly sent forward by express to me."—*Gov. Andrew's dispatch
to the Mayor of Baltimore.*

The *Miner's Journal* of Pottsville, Pa., furnishes the following
verses, which are as tenderly beautiful as that immortal poem,
The Bridge of Sighs, of which the style is an imitation :

Send them home tenderly;
    Guard them with care;
Eager eyes tearfully
    Watch for them there;
Home hearts are mournfully
    Throbbing to know
Gifted and manly sons,
    Stricken so low.

Send them home tenderly,
    To the fair sod,
First by the martyr-soul'd,
    Puritans trod;
Blue hill and ocean wave
    Echo the prayer—
" Send them home tenderly;
    Love waits them there !"

Send them home tenderly;
    Poor breathless clay !
Yet what high hopefulness
    Bore them away;
Hand to hand, clingingly,
    Linked in brave trust—
Tenderly, tenderly,
    Bear home their dust.

Send them home tenderly;
    Think of the sire,
Struggling with mighty sobs,
    By the low fire;

Think, how a mother's heart
    Hourly hath bled !
Tenderly, tenderly,
    Bear home her dead !

—Stella.

THE DEAD AT HOME.

[From *A Tale of* 1861, by Edw. Sprague Rand, Jr.]

I mind me when the honored dead in solemn pomp
    came home,
How our starry banner dropped half-mast on the
    high State House dome.
How minute guns spoke sharply out, and sad the
    the bells were tolling,
And mournfully upon the breeze the funeral dirge
    was rolling.

O there was that within the looks, within the eyes
    of men,
A stern determination, I never saw but then;
With hard pressed lips and swimming eyes they
    watched the funeral train,
With bowed, uncovered heads, they stood amid the
    falling rain.

In vision yet I seem to see the biers with flags en-
    twined,
The memory of that solemn dirge will never flee my
    mind;
And Massachusetts lifts her head more proudly at
    this day,
That twice in Freedom's battles her sons have led
    the way.

LAISSER ALLER.

BY FRANKLIN LUSHINGTON.

No more words;
Try it with your swords!
Try it with the arms of your bravest and your best!
You are proud of your manhood, now put it to the
test;
Not another word;
Try it by the sword.

No more *notes*;
Try it by the throats
Of the cannon that will roar till the earth and air
be shaken:
For they speak what they mean, and they cannot be
mistaken;
No more doubt;
Come—fight it out.

No child's play!
Waste not a day;
Serve out the deadliest weapons that you know;
Let them pitilessly hail on the faces of the foe;
No blind strife;
Waste not one life.

You that in the front
Bear the battle's brunt—
When the sun gleams at dawn on the bayonets
abreast,
Remember 'tis for government and country you con-
test;
For love of all you guard,
Stand and strike hard.

You at home that stay
From danger far away,
Leave not a jot to chance, while you rest in quiet
ease;

Quick! forge the bolts of death; quick! ship them
o'er the seas;
If war's feet are lame,
Yours will be the blame.

You my lads, abroad,
"Steady!" be your word:
You, at home, be the anchor of your soldiers young
and brave;
Spare no cost, none is lost, that may strengthen or
may save;
Sloth were sin and shame;
Now play out the game.
                              —Transcript.

OUR COUNTRY'S CALL.

BY WILLIAM CULLEN BRYANT.

Lay down the ax, fling by the spade;
Leave in its track the toiling plow;
The rifle and the bayonet blade
For arms like yours were fitter now;
And let the hands that ply the pen
Quit the light task, and learn to wield
The horseman's crooked brand, and rein
The charger on the battle-field.

Our Country calls; away! away!
To where the blood-stream blots the green,
Strike to defend the gentlest sway
That Time in all his course has seen.
See, from a thousand coverts—see
Spring the armed foes that haunt her track;
They rush to smite her down, and we
Must beat the banded traitors back.

Ho! sturdy as the oaks ye cleave
And moved as soon to fear and flight,
Men of the glade and forest! leave
Your woodcraft for the field of fight.

The arms that wield the ax must pour
  An iron tempest on the foe;
His serried ranks shall reel before
  The arm that lays the panther low.

And ye who breast the mountain storm
  By grassy steep or highland lake,
Come, for the land ye love to form
  A bulwark that no foe can break.
Stand, like your own gray cliffs that mock
  The whirlwind, stand in her defence;
The blast as soon shall move the rock
  As rushing squadron bear ye thence.

And ye, whose homes are by her grand
  Swift rivers, rising far away,
Come from the depth of her green land
  As mighty in your march as they;
As terrible as when the rains
  Have swelled them over bank and bourne,
With sudden floods to drown the plains
  And sweep along the woods uptorn.

And ye who throng, beside the deep,
  Her ports and hamlets on the strand,
In numbers like the waves that leap
  On the long murmuring marge of sand,
Come, like that deep, when o'er his brim,
  He rises all his floods to pour,
And flings the proudest barks that swim,
  A helpless wreck against his shore,

Few, few were they whose swords of old,
  Won the fair land in which we dwell;
But we are many, we who hold
  The grim resolve to guard it well.
Strike for that broad and goodly land,
  Blow after blow, till men shall see
That Might and Right move hand in hand,
  And glorious must their triumph be,

BAY STATE SONG.

"They had sent word to us from Philadelphia that we could not pass through that city (Baltimore), but the Colonel made up his mind that we could; and so we did. * * * * You may depend upon it, that wherever we are ordered, we shall do our duty, and not make a blot on the records of Massachusetts."—*Letter from a Private of the Sixth Regiment.*

"The cause of Baltimore is the cause of the whole south."—. *A. H. Stephens.*

TUNE—*There is rest for the weary* (with spirit).

'Tis the Old Bay State a-coming,
　　With the Pine Tree waving high,
Foremost where the fight is thickest,
　　Freedom still her battle-cry.
From the rocky shore of Plymouth,
　　From the plains of Lexington,
From beneath the shaft of Bunker,
　　Every hero sends a son.

Chorus.

To the fray comes the Bay State!
Clear the way for the Bay State!
Trust you may in the Bay State!
She will do, or die.

From our dear old Berkshire mountains,
　　From Cape Cod's sea-beaten strand,
With one cry we rush to battle—
　　Freedom, and our native Land!
From the quiet graves of Concord,
　　Still as in our fathers' day,
Where her country's need is greatest,
　　Massachusetts leads the way.

To the fray, &c.

Onward dash the Pine-Tree banner,
　　Where a threatened Senate calls,
Ere a Foe in Freedom's city
　　Desecrate her sacred halls.

Where a son would strike a mother
  With a traitor's stealthy blow,
Forward, every loyal brother!
  Fly to crush the dastard foe.
    To the fray &c.

Onward then our stainless banner,
  Let it kiss the stripe and star,
Till in weal and woe united
  They forever wedded are.
We will plant them by the river,
  By the gulf and by the strand,
Till they float, to float forever,
  O'er a free, united land.
    To the fray, &c.

We have left the plow and anvil,
  Left the ledger and the loom;
Our shares to swords are beaten,
  And our pen's the pen of doom.
But we'll plough a deeper furrow,
  And we'll deal a heavier blow,
And upon the Nation's Ledger
  We'll strike the balance now.
    To the fray, &c.

Lay the rails and build the engines,
  O'er the stream the bridges throw;
These are little Yankee notions
  Yankees carry as they go.
To the friends we leave behind us,
  Oft we pledge a hearty health,
And one prayer to God we offer—
  Save the good old Commonwealth.
    To the fray, &c.

See an Adams and an Otis
  Look from heaven to speed us on!
Hear a Warren and a Prescott
  Bid us keep the fields they won!

See again Virginia's Patriot
  Rise to bid Disunion stand!
See the shade of Monticello
  Strike again at Treason's hand!
     To the fray, &c.

Forward, then, the Pine-Tree banner!
  Still as in our fathers' day,
Where her country's need is greatest,
  Massachusetts leads the way!
By our brothers' blood still crying
  From the streets of Baltimore,
Let the foe who struck behind them,
  Be struck down for evermore.
     To the fray, &c.

Now, the Stars and Strips forever!
  Be he cursed, each traitor son,
Who assails the starry banner
  And the flag of Washington!
For Mount Vernon's sacred ashes
  Will not rest within their bed,
With a traitor band around it,
  And a traitor flag o'erhead!
     To the fray, &c.

                  —N. Y. Tribune.

PRO PATRIA.

[Inscribed to the Second New Hampshire Regiment.]

BY THOMAS BAILEY ALDRICH.

The grand old earth shakes at the tread of the
    Norsemen,
  Who meet, as of old, in defence of the true;
All hail to the stars that are set in their banner!
  All hail to the red, and the white, and the blue!
     As each column wheels by,
     Hear their hearts' battle-cry,—
It was Warren's,—'Tis sweet for our country to die!

Lancaster and Coos, Laconia and Concord,
   Old Portsmouth and Keene, send their stalwart
      young men;   [anvil,
They come from the plough, and the loom, and the
   From the marge of the sea, from the hill-top and
      glen.
        As each column wheels by,
   - Hear their hearts' battle-cry,—
It was Warren's—'Tis sweet for our country to die!

The prayers of fair women, like legions of angels,
   Watch over our soldiers by day and by night;
And the King of all Glory, the Chief of all Armies,
   Shall love them and lead them who dare to be
        As each column wheels by,   [right!
      Hear their hearts, battle-cry,—
It was Warren's,—'Tis sweet for our country to die!
                     —*N. Y. Tribune.*

CHEERS FOR THE BANNER.

Cheers for the banner as we rally 'neath its stars,
As we join the Northern legions, and are off for the
   wars,
Ready for the onset, bullet, blood, and scars,
        Cheers for the dear old flag.

Chorus.

     Glory! glory! glory to the North;
     Glory to the soldiers she is sending forth:
     Glory! glory! glory for the North;
        They will conquer as they go.

Cheers for the sweethearts we are now forced to
   leave :
Think of us, lassies, but for us don't you grieve;
Bright will be the garlands that you for us will
   weave
        When we return from the wars.
  2   Glory! &c.

Blank looks in Dixie when Northern troops come ;
Sad hearts in Dixie when they hear the victors'
    drum ;
Pale cheeks in Dixie, and rattle shell and bomb,
        And down goes the Dixie rag.
          Glory ! &c.

Swift heels in Dixie, but swifter on the track,
We'll meet them on their stumping grounds and
    quickly drive them back ;
Nimble heels in Dixie when they hear the rifles crack,
        Of the brave Green Mountain boys.
         Glory ! &c.

LITTLE RHODY.

Of all the true host that New England can boast,
    From down by the sea unto highland,
No State is more true, or more willing to do.
    Than dear little Yankee Rhode Island.
        Loyal and true little Rhody !
        Bully for you, little Rhody!
Governor Sprague was not very vague,
When he said, " Shoulder arms ! little Rhody ! "

Not backward at all at the President's call,
    Nor yet with the air of a toady,
The gay little State, not a moment too late,
    Sent soldiers to answer for Rhody.
        Loyal and true little Rhody !
        Bully for you, little Rhody !
Governor Sprague was not very vague,
When he said, " Shoulder arms ! little Rhody ! "

Two regiments raised, and by every one praised,
    Were soon on the march for head-quarters ;
All furnished first-rate at the cost of the State,
    And regular fighting dread-naughters !

Loyal and true little Rhody !
Bully for you, little Rhody !
Governor Sprague was not very vague,
When he said, " Shoulder arms ! little Rhody ! "

Let traitors look out, for there's never a doubt,
   That Uncle Abe's army will trip 'em ;
And as for the loud Carolinian crowd,
   Rhode Island alone, sir, can whip em!
      Loyal and true little Rhody !
      Bully for you, little Rhody!
Governor Sprague is a very good egg,
And worthy to lead little Rhody !
          —N. Y. Sunday Mercury.

ALL FORWARD!

WRITTEN FOR THE SECOND REGIMENT CONNECTICUT
VOLUNTEERS, BY REQUEST.

AIR—*Garibaldi's Hymn.*

All forward ! All forward !
All forward to battle ! the trumpets are crying,
Forward ! All forward ! our old flag is flying.
When Liberty calls us we linger no longer;
   Rebels, come on ! though a thousand to one !
Liberty ! Liberty ! deathless and glorious,
Under thy banner thy sons are victorious,
Free souls are valiant, and strong arms are stronger—
   God shall go with us and battle be won.
      Hurrah for the banner !
      Hurrah for the banner !
   Hurrah for our banner, the flag of the free !

      All forward ! All forward !
All forward for Freedom ! In terrible splendor
She comes to the loyal who die to defend her :
Her stars and her stripes o'er the wild wave of
   battle

Shall float in the heavens to welcome us on.
All forward! to glory, though life-blood is pouring,
Where bright swords are flashing, and cannon are
    roaring,
Welcome to death in the bullet's quick rattle—
    Fighting or falling shall freedom be won.
            Hurrah for the banner! &c.

        All forward! All forward!
All forward to conquer! Where free hearts are
    beating,
Death to the coward who dreams of retreating!
Liberty calls us from mountain and valley;
    Waving her banner, she leads to the fight.
Forward! all forward, the trumpets are crying;
The drum beats to arms, and the old flag is flying;
Stout hearts and strong hands around it shall
    rally—
    Forward to battle for God and the Right!
            Hurrah for the banner!
            Hurrah for the banner!
    Hurrah for our banner, the flag of the free!
                            —*The Independent.*

SONG OF THE SOLDIER.

Tune—*Shining Shore.*

The moon has set, the signal light
    Sends high its solemn warning!
We sleep upon our arms to-night
    And wait the battle morning.

Chorus.

    We march beneath the Stripes and Stars,
        God's banner! let earth bless it!
    Yet to it every knee shall bow,
        And every tongue confess it!

Again the signal light gleams forth,
  And hark! the " long roll " beating!
To arms! fall into line and give
  The foe a freeman's greeting.
     We march, &c.

If we fall on the battle-field,
  Friends, let there be no sighing;
There is in all the universe
  No better place for dying.
     We march, &c.

A few years more, a few years less,
  What matters it, my brother?
Our duty done—we'll fearless pass
  From this world to the other.
     We march, &c.

This thought shall sweeten life's last hour,
  Our Heavenly Father sees us;
Die humbly for the human race,
  As once died holy Jesus.
     We march, &c.

But see! red shot and hissing shell
  The Southern skies illuming!
And hark! the Northern answer, in
  The cannon's sullen booming.
     We march, &c.

Hurrah! the bugles sound the charge!
  O sturdy Northern yeoman!
With tempest stride and serried steel
  Sweep down upon the foeman!
     We march, &c.

The trampled of the distant lands
  Watch, pray and wonder!
The slaves shout in the barracoon
  As through the breach we thunder.
     We march, &c.

COLONEL ELLSWORTH.

BY CAPT. SAM. WHITING.

[Dedicated to the New York Fire Zouaves.]

Columbia bends in sadness now,
　　Above her gallant soldier's grave;
Laurel and cypress deck the brow
　　Of the dead Zouave—so young, so brave.
Cut down in manhood's brightest bloom—
　　Of his dear friends the hope and pride—
He sleeps within an honored tomb,
　　Who for his country bravely died.

Not yet in vain such heroes fall;
　　Their memory lives in every breast,
While streams of glory gild their pall,
　　And beautify their place of rest.
Oh! gallant Zouave, 'twas thy proud deed
　　To tear the rebel banner down;
Thy country gives the fitting meed—
　　A soldier's grave, a hero's crown.

Brave Fire Zouaves! your leader's name
　　Is left you for a battle-cry;
Let Ellsworth's pure and spotless fame
　　Lead you to conquer or to die.
Strike bravely when the *rebel rag*
　　Shall meet your eyes on Southern plain!
Strike! till Columbia's starry flag
　　O'er this whole land shall wave again.

When you shall meet the traitor band
　　Which seeks our Union to o'erthrow,
Strike boldly for our glorious land,
　　And call on God to nerve the blow!
Keep your dead Colonel e'er in view,
　　Wherever in this war you roam,
And let this shout your zeal renew:
　　" *Remember Ellsworth! Zouaves, strike home!* "
Hempstead.   —*N. Y. Tribune.*

THE MEN OF MARBLEHEAD.

[A Fact of April, 1861.]

BY R. W. RAYMOND.

It was the middle of the night,
   And deep was slumber's spell;
The sexton from the steeple's height
   Tolled loud the old church bell;
And quickly crowded young and old,
   Ere yet the echoes fell,
To hear the thrilling story told
   They knew before so well.

" What ho ! ye men of Marblehead,
   Who fought so well of yore !
Are all the fathers' virtues dead,
   And will they wake no more?
The traitor's hand hath dared to stain
   The starry flag ye bore :
Will ye not spring to draw again
   The swords ye drew before?"

The stalwart men of Marblehead
   Took down their guns and swords,
The weapons of the patriot dead
   Long gone to be the Lord's;
They kissed their sweethearts and their wives,
   With few and tender words;
They went, to hurl a thousand lives
   Upon the Southern hordes !

'Twas midnight when the summons came:
   The morn his chariot sped,
And glancing with an eye of flame
   Across the ocean bed,
Saw bright the well-known colors play—
   The blue, and white, and red—
And steel gleam through the morning gray
Where grimly trod the Southward way
   The men of Marblehead.

All hail, thou Banner of the Stars !
  Long may thy colors fly!
Thou ledst our fathers to the wars;
  We will not cast thee by!
No ! let the soil grow crimson red,
  And lurid flash the sky,
With thy fair folds above us spread,
Like the brave men of Marblehead,
  We'll conquer, or we'll die !.

THE DRUMMER BOY OF MARBLEHEAD.

BY CARRIE CARLETON.

Where the billows dash with sullen roar,
Throwing their spray on the sandy shore,
Many a fond heart, loyal and brave,
Sleeps to the song of the moaning wave.

Could we give a voice to the sea shells fair
Or a pen to the green weeds clinging there,
Many a hero, now lost to fame,
Might gain for the loss of life, a name.

Here lieth one with silvery hair,
Another in youthful beauty there;
But loveliest in all that crowd of dead
Lay the Drummer Boy of Marblehead.

Bright as the sunlight, and free from care,
As the birds that sport in summer air ;
Brave as the bravest, make soft his bed
For the Drummer Boy of Marblehead.

Lay him down tenderly,—never more
May the hero-boy enter his mother's door ;
For fatal the leaden message sped
To the Drummer Boy of Marblehead.

Could ye not spare *him* of all beside?
Joy of his Mother—his Father's pride!
Could ye not rest with the others, dead,
Without the fair boy of Marblehead?

A curse on the traitorous hands that strove
Our country's flag and fame to rive,
Ay, a curse on the hands whose bullet sped
To the Drummer Boy of Marblehead.
—*The Voice.*

TO ARMS!

BY MARTHA PERRY LOWE.

Traitors and foes! We shall arm! We shall arm!
  Brethren, are ye—but it matters us not—
Men of the South! We are calm! We are calm!
  You are like madmen, misguided and hot!

Long have we patiently borne with your hate;
  Shame has been rising and flushing our brow;
Oh we have entreated you early and late—
  God only knows what has come o'er us now!

We are not angry, the fire is too deep,
  We shall not taunt—that's for boys, and not men;
Yet we have sworn, and our word we will keep,
  Never shall you trample on us again!

You have dishonored the stripes and the stars!
  The pale North a moment, *did* hold in her breath,
Now thousands of eyes like the red planet Mars,
  Do glare on you steady, defiance and death!

Lord of the Nations! Restrain us! Restrain!
  Terrible, mighty our waking will be;
Blood when it flows will come down like rain,
  Flooding the earth like the surge of the sea.
3

COMING.

BY ALICE CAREY.

They are mustering—they are marching !
  How their onward tramping rolls !
The are coming, coming, coming !
  A hundred thousand souls !

From the granite hills—the seaside,
  In solid ranks like walls—
A hundred men to take the place
  Of every man that falls.

Right on, across the midnight—
  Right onward, stern and proud—
Their red flags shining as they come,
  Like morning on a cloud.

Battalion on battalion,
  The West its bravery pours,
For the colors God's own hand has set,
  In the bushes at their doors !

In the woods and in the clearings,
  The lovers, brothers, sons,
The young men and the old men
  Are shouldering their guns.

They have heard the bugle blowing—
  Heard the thunder of the drum,
And farther than the eye can see—
  They come, and come, and come!

"CALL ALL ! CALL ALL !"

[A Rebel War Song.]

Whoop ! the Doodles have broken loose,
Roaring round like the fiery duce !
Lice of Egypt, a hungry pack:
After 'em, boys, and drive 'em back !

Bull dog, terrier, cur and fice,
Back to the beggarly land of ice;
Worry 'em, bite 'em, scratch and tear,
Everybody and everywhere.

Old Kentucky's caved from under;
Tennessee is split asunder;
Alabama awaits attack,
And Georgia bristles at her back.

Old John Brown is dead and gone!
Still his spirit is marching on,
Lantern-jawed, and legs, my boys,
Long as an Ape's from Illinois.

Want a weapon?   Gather a brick !
Club or cudgel, or stone or stick ;
Anything with a blade or butt;
Anything that can cleave or cut.

Anything heavy, or hard, or keen !
Any sort of a slaying machine;
Anything with a willing mind
And the steady arm of a man behind.

Want a weapon?   Why, capture one!
Every Doodle has got a gun,
Belt and bayonet, bright and new,
Kill a Doodle, and capture TWO!

Shoulder to shoulder, son and sire !
All! call all! to the feast of fire !
Mother and maiden, and child and slave,
A common triumph, or a single grave !
                    —*Harrisonburg, Virginia.*

THE SOUTH CAROLINA GENTLEMAN.

TUNE—*The Fine Old English Gentleman.*

Down in a small Palmetto State the curious ones
    may find,
A ripping, tearing gentleman of an uncommon kind.

A staggering, swaggering sort of chap, who takes
    his whiskey straight,
And frequently condemns his eyes to that ultimate
    vengeance which a clergyman of high standing
    has assured must be a sinner's fate;
This South Carolina gentleman, one of the present
    time.

You trace his genealogy, and not far you'll see,
A most undoubted Octoroon, or mayhap a mustee;
And if you note the shaggy locks that cluster on his
    brow,
You'll find that every other hair is varied with a
    kink that seldom denotes pure Caucasian blood,
    but on the contrary betrays an admixture with
    a race not particularly popular now,
This South Carolina gentleman, one of the present
    time.

He always wears a full dress coat, pre-Adamite in
    cut,
With waistcoat of the broadest style, through which
    his ruffles jut,
Six breast pins deck his horrid front, and on his
    fingers shine
Whole invoices of diamond rings, which could hardly
    pass muster with the original Jacobs in Chatham
    street for jewels genuine,
This South Carolina gentleman, one of the present
    time.

He chews tobacco by the pound, and spits upon the
    floor,
If there is not a box of sand behind the nearest door;
And when he takes a weekly spree he clears a mighty
    track
Of everything that bears the shape of whiskey-skin,
    gin and sugar—brandy sour, peach and honey,
    irrepressible cocktail, rum and gum and luscious
    apple-jack,

This South Carolina gentleman, one of the present
time.

He takes to euchre kindly, too, and plays an awful
hand,
Especially when those he tricks his style don't under-
stand;
And if he wins, why then he stops to pocket all the
stakes,
But if he loses, then he says to the unfortunate
stranger who has chanced to win: "Its my
opinion that you are a cursed Abolitionist, and
if you don't leave South Carolina in one hour,
you will be hung like a dog,"—but no offer to
pay the loss he make,
This South Carolina gentleman, one of the present
time.

Of course he's all the time in debt to those who
credit give,
Yet manages upon the best the market yields to live,
But if a Northern creditor ask him his bill to heed,
This honorable gentleman instantly draws his bowie
knives and a pistol, dons a blue cockade, and
declares that in consequence of the repeated
aggressions of the North, and its gross viola-
tions of the Constitution, he feels that it would
utterly degrade him to pay any debt whatever,
and that in fact he had determined to SECEDE.
This South Carolina gentleman, one of the present
kind.

REPUDIATION.

'Neath a ragged palmetto a Southerner sat,
A twisting the band of his Panama hat,
And trying to lighten his mind of a load
By humming the words of the following ode:

" Oh ! for a nigger, and oh ! for a whip;
  Oh ! for a cocktail, and oh ! for a nip;
  Oh ! for a shot at old Greeley and Beecher;
  Oh ! for a crack at a Yankee school teacher;
  Oh ! for a captain, and oh ! for a ship ;
  Oh ! for a cargo of niggers each trip."
And so he kept oh-ing for all he had not,
Not contented with owing with all that he'd got.

—Orpheus C. Kerr Papers.

"ALL WE ASK IS TO BE LET ALONE."

As vonce I valked by a dismal swamp,
There sat an old Cove in the dark and damp,
And at everybody as passed that road
A stick or a stone this old Cove throwed.
And venever he flung his stick or his stone,
He'd set up a song of " Let me alone ! '

Let me alone, for I loves to shy
These bits of things at the passers by—
Let me alone, for I've got your tin,
And lots of other traps snugly in,
Let me alone, I'm riggin' a boat
To grab votever you've got afloat—
In a veek or so I expect to come
And turn you out of your ouse and ome—
I'm a quiet old Cove," says he with a groan,
" All I axes is—Let me alone!"

Just then came along on the self-same vay,
Another old Cove, and begand for to say—
" Let you alone ! That's comin' it strong!
You've been let alone—a darn'd sight too long—
Of all the sarce that ever I heerd,
Put down that stick ! (you may well looked skeered,)
Let go that stone ! If you once show fight,
I'll knock you higher than any kite.

You must have a lesson to stop your tricks,
And cure you of shying them stones and sticks,
And I'll have my hardware back and my cash,
And knock your scow into tarnal smash.
And if ever I catches you 'round my ranch,
I'll string you up to the nearest branch.
The best you can do is to go to bed,
And keep a decent tongue in your head;
For I reckon before you and I are done,
You'll wish you had let honest folks alone."

The old Cove stopped, and the t'other old Cove,
He sot quite still in his cypress grove,
And he looked at his stick revolvin' slow,
Vether 'twere safe to shy it or no—
And he grumbled on in an injured tone,
"All that I axed vos—Let me alone !"
—*Hartford Courant.*

"THUS SAITH THE LORD, I OFFER THEE THREE THINGS."

BY OLIVER WENDELL HOLMES.

In poisonous dens, where traitors hide
  Like bats that fear the day,
While all the land our charters claim
Is sweating blood and breathing flame,
Dead to their country's wo and shame,
  The recreants whisper, STAY!

In peaceful homes, where patriot fires
  On Love's own altars glow,
The mother hides her trembling fear,
The wife, the sister checks a tear,
To breathe the parting word of cheer,
  Soldier of Freedom, Go!

In halls where luxury lies at ease,
  And Mammon keeps his state,

Where flatterers fawn and menials crouch,
The dreamer, startled from his couch,
Wrings a few counters from his pouch,
    And murmurs faintly, WAIT !

In weary camps, on trampled plains
    That ring with fife and drum,
The battling host, whose harness gleams
Along the crimson-flowing streams,
Calls, like a warning voice in dreams,
    We want you, Brother, COME !

Choose ye whose bidding ye will do—
    To go, to wait, to stay!
Sons of the Freedom loving town,
Heirs of the Fathers' old renown,
The servile yoke, the civic crown
    Await your choice TO-DAY !

The stake is laid !   O gallant youth
    With yet unsilvered brow,
If Heaven should lose and Hell should win,
On whom should lie the mortal sin,
Whose record is, IT MIGHT HAVE BEEN ?
    God calls you—answer, NOW !

SCOTT AND THE VETERAN.

BY BAYARD TAYLOR.

An old and crippled veteran to the War Department
    came ;
He sought the Chief who led him on many a field of
    fame—
The Chief who shouted " Forward !" where'er his
    banner rose,
And bore its stars in triumph behind the flying foes.
" Have you forgotten, General," the battered soldier
    cried,

"The days of Eighteen Hundred Twelve, when I
was at your side ?
Have you forgotten Johnson, that fought at Lundy's
Lane ?
'Tis true, I'm old and pensioned, but I want to fight
again."

"Have I forgotten ?' said the Chief; "my brave
old soldier, No !
And here's the hand I gave you then, and let it tell
you so ;
But you have done your share, my friend ; you're
crippled, old, and gray,
And we have need of younger arms and fresher blood
to-day.''

" But, General," cried the veteran, a flush upon his
brow,
'' The very men who fought with us, they say, are
traitors now ;
They've torn the flag of Lundy's Lane—our old red,
white and blue ;
And while a drop of blood is left, I'll show that
blood is true.

'' I'm not so weak but I can strike, and I've a good
old gun
To get the range of traitors' hearts, and pick them,
one by one.
Your Minie rifles, and such arms, it aint worth while
to try ;
I couldn't get the hang of them, but I'll keep my
powder dry !''

" God bless you, comrade !" said the Chief; " God
bless your loyal heart !
But younger men are in the field, and claim to have
their part ;

They'll plant our sacred banner in each rebellious
    town,
And woe, henceforth, to any hand that dares to pull
    it down!"

"But General,"—still persisting, the weeping vete-
    ran cried,
"I'm young enough to follow, so long as *you're* my
    guide ;
And some, you know, must bite the dust, and that,
    at least, can I ;
So, give the young ones place to fight, but me a
    place to die !

"If they should fire on Pickens, let the Colonel in
    command
Put me upon the rampart, with the flag staff in my
    hand ;
No odds how hot the cannon-smoke, or how the
    shells may fly ;
I'll hold the Stars and Stripes aloft, and hold them
    till I die !

"I'm ready, General, so you let a post to me be
    given,
Where Washington can see me, as he looks from
    highest heaven,
And say to Putnam at his side, or,-may-be, General
    Wayne,
'There stands old Billy Johnson, that fought at
    Lundy's Lane ! '

"And when the fight is hottest, before the traitors
    fly,
When shell and ball are screeching, and bursting in
    the sky,
If any shot should hit me, and lay me on my face,
My soul would go to Washington, and not to Arnold's
    place !"

                                        —The Independent.

ALL OF THEM.

A blacksmith of Brooklyn, N. Y., and his four sons, have enlisted during the war in the 14th Regiment.—*Tribune.*

With head erect, and lips compressed,
    He throws his hammer by ;
The purpose of his manly breast
    Is now to do or die.

He seeks the camp : "Put down my name,
    (My boys will mind the shop);
If the traitors' want my heart's best blood,
    I'll sell it drop for drop.

" And here comes now my oldest boy :
    My son what would you do ? "
" Father, my brother will drive the trade ;
    I've come to fight with you."

" God bless him ! well, put down his name,
    I cannot send him home.
But here's the other boy, I see :
    My son, what made you come ? "

" Father, I could not work alone ;
    The shop may go to—grass ;
I've come to fight for the good old flag ;
    Stand off here—let me pass."

" Yes, put him down—he's a noble boy ;
    I've two that are younger still ;
They'll drive the plow on the Flushing farm,
    And work with a right good will.

" My God ! and here comes one of them !
    My son, you must not go ! "
" Father, when traitors are marching on,
    I cannot plow or sow ! "

" Well, thank God, there is one left yet ;
    He will plow and sow what he can,

But he's only a boy, and can never do
    The work of a full-grown man.''

With a proud, full heart, the blacksmith turned,
    And walked to the other side,
For he felt a weakness he almost scorned,
    And a tear he fain would hide.

They told him then, his youngest boy
    Was putting his name on the roll :
" It must not be,'' said the brave old man ;
    '' No, no, he's the light of my soul ! ''

But the lad came up with a beaming face,
    Which bore neither fears nor cares :
'' Father, say nothing—my name is down ;
    I have let out the farm on shares.''

And now they've marched to the tented field,
    And when the wild battle shall come,
They'll strike a full blow for the stars and stripes,
    For God, and their Country, and Home.

THE YOUNG VOLUNTEER'S GOOD-BYE.

BY J. HAL. ELLIOT.

Come up to my little chamber, mother,
    Come and bless me before I sleep,
'Tis the last night I'll be here, you know,
    And it will do me good to weep.

I have said good-bye to the rest, mother,
    I have parted with all but you,
And the great hot tears fell thick and fast,
    But the words that we spoke were few.

And my heart aches with the parting, mother,
    " God bless you!" was all that they said,
With quivering lips and wistful eyes,
    As tho' I were already dead.

So come to my little chamber, mother,
  As you used to come long ago,
When the twilight shades were gathering,
  And the West was all aglow.

You remember those hallowed times, mother,
  When we used to kneel side by side,
While you prayed to God so earnestly,
  That your little boy sobbed and cried.

I want you to pray with me now, mother,
  With your arms wound around me tight,
Pray God to protect and keep me safe,
  And to make me brave in the fight.

Thir war is a horrible thing, mother,
  I shudder to think of it so,
That visions of blood sweep past my brain,
  Till my soul seems flooded with woe.

But my country calls for me now, mother,
  It calls for me almost by name,
And I cannot stay at home in peace,
  When her flag is trampled in shame.

I shall fight to the very death, mother,
  For our cause is righteous, I know,
I shall fight till the Stars and Stripes once more
  Float as pure and spotless as snow.

So pray to God with your whole soul, mother,
  As you used in the days gone by —
And it will not shame my manhood now,
  If I lean on your breast and cry.

If I come back to you again, mother,
  You'll be glad I went to the fight,
For a victor's crown upon my brow,
  Will answer your prayer of to-night.

If I fall on the field of battle, mother,
  You will know that I died for the Right,
And your heart will be glad while you weep,
  When you think of our good-bye to-night.

Now here in my little chamber, mother,
  With my head pillowed on your breast,
I'll whisper my last good-bye to you,
  And prayerfully go to my rest.

I'm off with the early sunrise, mother,
  I shall leave you all asleep—
There are stirring times ahead for us all,
  I have no more time to weep.
Blackstone, Mass., July, 1861.

THE VOLUNTEER'S MOTHER.

He is my boy, my only boy,
  His father died long years gone by;
And little have I known of joy
  But gazing on his dark blue eye.
'Tis lighted now with higher glow;
His country calls him; let him go!

He never grieved me; tender, kind, ·
  Strong, loving—full of hope and grace—
My life was in his own entwined,
  My heart but mirrored back his face.
With stern resolve he seeks the foe;
His country calls him; let him go!

How oft I have sat beside
  Him sleeping—clustring round his head
Those rich brown locks, my praise, my pride!
  And now the earth must be his bed.
'Tis wrong to grieve for this. I know;
His country calls him; let him go!

Ah! in how many hearts this strife
　Is waged in prayer, by prayer is won!
There is the wood, the fire, the knife,
　And for the sacrifice—our son!
'Twould kill me if he fell; but no!
His country calls him; let him go!

For God, who gave our land so blest,
　Would have us guard it; heart and home
Give up their best at such behest.
　The gulf was closed in heathen Rome
With one young warrior.　Weal or woe,
His country calls him; let him go!

————

DEBORAH KING.

Come, women! pray for a woman!
　She has done what she could, she's a mother!
She has given up that all she had,
　This mite of a man is no other
　　Than Clermont.　Who's Clermont? her lad!

Not twenty-one yet, to be sure, sir,
　But he is eighteen, sir, and over!
And as brave, sir, and strong as young David,
　He'll fight like a lion or lover.

In black and white there, if you're eager!
　Quaint characters wrought out of pain.
How earnest and honest this leader!
　But—glad! there's a blot and a stain.

"This Clermont," she writes, "I've no other—
　He's mine, my one son, and he'll bring　.
The consent that you want, I'm his mother."
　Signed valiantly "Deborah King."

But here's only one name, just "the woman's,
    There's another must sign it," they said.
Clermont King flashed the fire of old Romans
    Into speech, " for my father is dead.'
        Living father ! consent for the son !

In the long hot forced marches support him !
    In the dark day of overthrow, shield!
Let officer never report him,
    A private left dead on the field.

Pray, women, for Deborah's son !
    Christ save him from sun-stroke and fever.
Save Clermont, this widow's one son !
    We are thinking of Nain, Lord; remember
Her glory when peace shall be won.
Canandaigua, N. Y.

THE WIFE'S SONG.

BY KATE CAMERON.

Some give to our country their talents and time,
    And others give their gold;
I had only one treasure to bestow,
    And that I did not withhold.
And I know the offering will be blest,
    For, oh, it was my all:
God pity me, if in battle hour
    It should be *his* fate to fall !

I have given my all to my country's call,
    And what more can I do?
I have given the strong arm on which I leaned,
    And the heart so brave and true.
Now I walk alone through the crowded streets,
    And alone I kneel to pray;
Ah, many a wearisome hour have I,
    With my loved one far away.

I know not if he will come back again;
　It may be my doom to see,
As so many have seen, in the fatal list,
　The one name that's dear to me.
But I trust him with One who is greater than all
　More loving and more kind;
Oh, God! defend those who have gone forth,
　And strengthen those left behind.
　　　　　　　　　—*Springfield Republican.*

GONE.

BY CHAUNCEY HICKOX.

Two voices murmuring tender talk,
　Two young cheeks touching, warm and sweet;
　Two mouths like dewy roses meet,
Down the dim borders of the walk.

One face of bronze and one of snow—
　And silent as their mingled breath,
　Tender and sad as love and death,
A thousand wordless blessings flow.

At last a slender arm withdrawn,
　At last two proud heads bowed; in vain
　Those fond lips try to speak again,
And through the darkness one has gone.

Round whose red way the bolts shall sing,
　And sweet to his bold heart and brain
　As robins' songs through April rain,
The stormy notes of battle ring.

And, ah! to one forever lies,
　Through change of years, and life, and place,
　The outline of a cold dead face
Upturned beneath the southern skies.

Camp Warren, Charleston, Va.　—*Cincinnati Commercial.*

4

THE BRAVE AT HOME.

BY T. BUCHANAN REED.

The maid who binds her warrior's sash,
　With smile that well her pain dissembles,
The while beneath her drooping lash
　One starry tear-drop hangs and trembles,
Tho' heaven alone records the tear,
　And Fame shall never know her story,
Her heart has shed a drop as dear
　As ever dewed the field of glory.

The wife who girds her husband's sword,
　'Mid little ones who weep or wonder,
And bravely speaks the cheering word,
　What tho' her heart be rent asunder—
Doomed nightly in her dreams to hear
　The bolts of war around him rattle,
Hath shed as sacred blood as e'er
　Was poured upon the plain of battle!

The mother who conceals her grief,
　While to her breast her son she presses,
Then breathes a few brave words and brief,
　Kissing the patriot brow she blesses.
With no one but her secret God
　To know the pain that weighs upon her,
Sheds holy blood as e'er the sod
　Received on Freedom's field of honor.

"ALONG THE LINES."

Oh, the eyes that are watching the river's shores,
　The river that gleams and shines,
Where our bravest and truest brothers now,
　Are watching along the lines.

Waiting wearily, too, are we,
　Waiting the fate-hour's chimes,
That shall awaken the din and roar
　Of battle, along the lines.

But hearts beat calmly, hearts beat slow,
  'Twill be redder than blood of vines, .
That Liberty's sacramental wine
  That shall flow along the lines.

And drearier than the solemn sighing
  Of winter among the pines,
Shall come the moanings of the dying
  To us from along the lines,

Ah well! that to-night the white tents gleam,
  Where the moonbeam flickers and shines,
And over the land the tidings come,
  " All quiet along the lines."

Only one prayer in the hush goes up
  To the innermost shrine of shrines:
" Success for our banner, wherever it streams
  In battle, along the lines."

ON GUARD.

The following lines were written by HENRY M. HUNT, à Massachusetts soldier in the 10th regiment, who died in Jan., 1862. He was a dutiful son and affectionate brother, and these lines were sent to his home but a short time previous to his death :

At midnight, on my lonely beat,
  When shadow wraps the wood and lea,
A vision seems my view to greet
  Of one at home who prays for me.

No roses blow upon her cheek—
  Her form is not a lover's dream—
But on her face so fair and meek,
  A host of holier beauties gleam.

For softly shines her silver hair,
  A patient smile is on her face,
And the mild, lustrous light of prayer
  Around her sheds a moon-like grace.

She prays for one that's far away—
    The soldier in his holy fight—
And begs that Heaven in mercy may
    Protect her boy and bless the Right !

Till, though the leagues lie far between,
    This silent incense of her heart
Steals o'er my soul, with breath serene,
    And we no longer are apart.

So guarding thus my lonely beat,
    By shadowy wood and haunted lea,
That vision seems my view to greet
    Of her at home who prays for me.

ALL QUIET ALONG THE POTOMAC.

A printed copy of the following beautiful lines was found in the pocket of one of our volunteers who died in camp upon the Potomac.

" All quiet along the Potomac," they say,
    " Except, now and then, a stray picket
Is shot, as he walks on his beat to and fro,
    By a rifleman hid in the thicket.
'Tis nothing—a private or two, now and then,
    Will not count in the news of the battle;
Not an officer lost, only one of the men
    Moaning out, all alone, the death rattle."

All quiet along the Potomac to-night,
    Where the soldiers lie peacefully dreaming;
Their tents in the rays of the clear autumn moon,
    Or the light of the watchfire, are gleaming.
A tremulous sigh as the gentle night wind
    Through the forest leaves softly creeping ;
While stars up above, with their glittering eyes,
    Keep guard—for the Army is sleeping.

There's only the sound of the lone sentry's tread,
　As he tramps from the rock to the fountain,
And thinks of the two in the low trundle bed,
　Far away in the cot on the mountain.
His musket falls slack—his face, dark and grim,
　Grows gentle with memories tender,
As he mutters a prayer for the children asleep—
　For their mother, may Heaven defend her !

The moon seems to shine just as brightly as then,
　That night when the love yet unspoken
Leaped up to his lips, and when low murmured vows
　Were pledged, to be ever unbroken.
Then drawing his sleeve roughly over his eyes,
　He dashes off tears that are welling,
And gathers his gun closer up to his place
　As if to keep down the heart-swelling.

He passes the fountain, the blasted pine tree,
　The footstep is lagging and weary;
Yet onward he goes through the broad belt of light
　Towards the shades of a forest so dreary.
Hark ! was it the nightwind that rustled the leaves ?
　Was it moonlight so wondrously flashing ?
It looked like a rifle—" Ha !—Mary, good bye !"
　And the life blood is ebbing and plashing.

All quiet along the Potomac to-night,
　No sound save the rush of the river;
While soft falls the dew on the face of the dead,—
　The picket's off duty, forever !

PICAYUNE BUTLER.

" General Butler was a barber."
　So the Pelicans were raving ;
Now you've got him in your harbor,
　Tell us how you like his shaving.

LOYAL DELAWARE.

In all the range of Border States,
 To whom we've ne'er been crusty,
The staunch, unflinching Delaware's
 The only one that's trusty.

While wicked Treason rages wild
 All up and down her borders,
She still defends the Stars and Stripes,
 And waits for further orders.

Not all Virginia's treachery,
 Nor Maryland's distraction,
Can make her quit her Uncle Sam,
 For any traitor faction.

And Delaware has had her share
 Of treason-agitators ;
But then there's something in her soil
 That don't agree with traitors.

The Union will remember her,
 When force of arms it uses,
And give to her of Maryland
 As much as e'er she chooses !

And when to future Peace we pledge
 A bumper, rare and royal,
We'll say of gallant Delaware,
 " She's little, but she's loyal ! "
    —*N. Y. Sunday Mercury.*

———

BULL RUN—Sunday, July 21.

BY ALICE B. HAVEN.

We—walking so slowly adown the green lane,
 With Sabbath-bells chiming, and birds singing
  psalms,

He—eager with haste, pressing on o'er the slain,
 'Mid the trampling of steeds and the drum-beat
  to arms,
   In that cool, dewy morning.

We—waiting with faces all reverent and still,
 The organ's voice vibrant with praise unto God ;
His face set like flint with the impress of will,
 To press back the foe, or to die on the sod—
  My fair, brave young brother !

We—kneeling to hear benedictions of love,
 Our hearts all at peace with the message from
  Heaven !
He—stretched on the field, gasping, wounded, to
  prove,
 If mercy were found where such courage had
  striven,
   In the midst of the slaughter.

O God !—can I live with the horrible truth !
 Stabbed through as he lay, with their glittering
  steel ;
Could they look in that face, like a woman's for
  youth,
 And crush out its beauty with musket and heel,
  Like hounds, or like demons !

That brow I have blessed in my dead mother's place,
 Each morning and evening since she went unto
  rest ;
Smoothing down the fair cheek, as my own baby's
  face,
 Those eyes with her look, where my kisses were
  prest,
   For I saw hers—so tender.

Curses spring to my lips ! Oh, my God, send the
 .   hail
 Of swift ready vengeance for deeds such as this!

Forego all thy mercy, if judgment must fail !
   Forgive my wild heart if it prayeth amiss—
      His blood crieth upward !

" Amiss ! "—and the strife of my clamorous grief
   Is hushed into stillness—what grief like to thine!
If my poor human heart, with its passions so brief,
   Is tortured with pangs, can we guess the Divine !
      With depths past all searching !

I know eyes more tender looked upward to Thee ;
   That visage, so marred with the torturing crown—
Those smooth, noble limbs, racked with anguish I
   see ;
   The side where the blood and the water gushed
   down,
      From stroke fierce and brutal.

Help lips white with anguish to take up his prayer;
   Help hearts that are bursting to stifle their cries;
The shout of the populace, too, has been there,
   To drown pleas for justice, to clothe truth in
   lies—
      To enrage and to madden.

They knew not we loved them; they knew not we
   prayed
   For their weal as our own ;—" we are brethren,"
   we plead ;
Unceasing those prayers to Our Father were made ;
   When they flung down the palm for palmetto, we
   said,
      " Let us still hope to win them."

" God so loved, that He gave ! " We are giving to
   these
The lives that were dearer to us than our own ;
Let us add prayer for blood, trusting God to appease
   Our heart's craving pain, when he hears on his
   throne,
      " Oh, Father forgive them !"
                  —*N. Y. Evening Post.*

WHO'S READY.

BY EDNA DEAN PROCTOR.

God help us ! who's ready? there's danger before !
Who's armed and who's mounted? the foe's at the
    door !
The smoke of his cannon hangs black o'er the plain;
His shouts ring exultant while counting our slain;
And Northward and Northward he presses his line—
Who's ready? O forward ! for yours and for mine !

No halting, no discord, the moments are Fates;
To shame or to glory they open the gates !
There's all we hold dearest to lose or to win;
The web of the future to-day we must spin;
And bid the hours follow with knell or with chime,
Who's ready? O forward ! while yet there is time !

Lead armies or councils—be soldier afield
Alike, so your valor is liberty's shield !
Alike, so you strike when the bugle-notes call,
For country, for fireside, for freedom to all !
The blows of the boldest will carry the day—
Who's ready? O forward ! there's death in delay !

Earth's noblest are praying, at home and o'er sea,
" God keep the great nation united and free ! "
Her tyrants watch, eager to leap at our life
If once we should falter or faint in the strife;
Our trust is unshaken, though legions assail—
Who's ready? O forward ! and right shall prevail !

Who's ready? " All ready ! " undaunted we cry;
" For country, for Freedom, we'll fight till we die !
No traitor, at midnight, shall pierce us in rest:
No alien, at noonday, shall stab us abreast;
The God of our Fathers is guiding us still—
All forward ! we're ready, and conquer we will ! "

THE SEVENTY-NINTH.

BY THOS. FRAZER.

AIR—*Here's to the year that's awa'.*

Come, muster, my bonnie brave Scots,
    An' muster your clans one an' a'
Nor heed who else lags, so the free Thistle wags,
    When Treason drives Right to the wa';
    For Freedom, for Union, an' Law,
      We'll do a' that true men may dare;
An' come weal or come scaithe, for these to the
      death—
    The Seventy-ninth will be there!

Comes stir, then, an' trim for the work;
    Come, Borderer, Lowlander, Celt,
An' wi' firelock in hand, our tartan-clad band
    Will soon mak the auld grit be felt.
    We'll show how auld Scotland for Truth
      Has bluid in her heart yet to spare;
An' let us but ken when the Truth may want men—
    The Seventy-ninth will be there !

Then heeze out the pipes wi' a cheer,
    An' up wi' some heart-thrillin' strain,
To mind us the field is where Scots never yield,
    While ae chance to win may remain.
    Syne shout, lads, the auld battle-cry—
      " Saint Andrew !"—an' let them beware
When doure Southron knaves wad mak North-folk
      their slaves—
    The Seventy-ninth will be there !

The Union, the Nation, an' Name,
    The " Stars and the Stripes," an' the Laws !
Oh ! never can hand wave the death-dealing brand
    In what could be holier cause !

Then muster, my bonnie brave Scots,
 An' swear by the tartan we wear,
Where'er be the van, one in heart to a man—
 The Seventy-ninth will be there !
                    —*N. Y. Commercial Advertiser.*

SONG OF THE IRISH LEGION.

BY JAMES DE MILLE.

E Pluribus Unum.   Erin go Bragh.

Ye boys of the sod, to Columbia true,
Come up, lads, and fight for the Red, White and
 Blue!
Two countries we love, and two mottoes we'll share,
And we'll join them in one on the banner we bear:
 Erin, mavourneen! Columbia, agra !
 E pluribus unum.   Erin go bragh.

Upon them, my lads! and the rebels shall know
How Erin can fight when she faces the foe;
If they can't give us arms, sure we needn't delay;
With a sprig of shillelagh we'll open the way.
 Erin, mavourneen! &c.

" Blood Tubs" and " Plug Uglies," and others
 galore,
Are sick for a thrashing in sweet Baltimore;
Be Jabers! that same I'd be proud to inform
Of the terrible force of an Irishman's arm.
 Erin, mavourneen! &c.

Before you the tyrant assembles his band,
And threatens to conquer this glorious land;
But it wasn't for this that we traversed the sea,
And left the Geen Isle for the land of the free.
 Erin, mavourneen! &c.

Go forth to the tyrant, and give him to know
That an Irishman holds him his bitterest foe;
And his sweetest delight is to meet him in fight,
To battle for freedom, with God for the right!
    Erin, mavourneen! &c.

THE FLOWER OF LIBERTY.

BY OLIVER WENDELL HOLMES.

What flower is this that greets the morn,
Its hues from heaven so freshly born?
With burning star and flaming brand
It kindles all the sunset land:
O, tell us what its name may be!
Is this the Flower of Liberty?
    It is the banner of the free,
    The starry Flower of Liberty!

In savage nature's far abode
Its tender seed our fathers sowed;
The storm-winds rocked its swelling bud,
Its opening leaves were streaked with blood
Till, lo! earth's tyrants shook to see
The full-blown Flower of Liberty!
    Then hail the banner of the free,
    The starry Flower of Liberty!

Behold its streaming rays unite
One mingling flood of braided light—
The red that fires the Southern rose,
With spotless white from Northern snows,
And spangled o'er its azure, see
The sister Stars of Liberty!
    Then hail, &c.

The blades of heroes fence it round;
Where'er it springs is holy ground;
From tower and dome its glories spread;
It waves where lonely sentries tread;

It makes the land as ocean free,
And plants an empire on the sea!
   Then hail, &c.

Thy sacred leaves, fair freedom's flower,
Shall ever float on dome and tower,
To all their heavenly colors true,
In blackening frost or crimson dew;
And God love us as we love thee,
Thrice holy Flower of Liberty!
    Then hail, &c.

LYON.

Sing, bird, on green Missouri plain,
  The saddest song of sorrow;
Drop tears, O clouds, in gentlest rain
  Ye from the wind can borrow;
Breathe out, ye winds, your softest sigh,
  Weep, flowers, in dewy splendor,
For him who knew well how to die,
  But not how to surrender.

Uprose serene the August sun
  Upon that day of glory;
Upcurled from musket and from gun
  The war cloud gray and hoary;
It gathered like a funeral pall,
  Now broken and now blended,
Where rang the bugle's angry call,
  And rank with rank contended.

Four thousand men as brave and true
  As e'er went forth in daring,
Upon the foe that morning threw
  The strength of their despairing.

They feared not death—men bless the field
    That patriot soldier died on—
Fair Freedom's cause was sword and shield,
    And at their head was Lyon.

Their leader's troubled soul looked forth
    From eyes of troubled brightness;
Sad soul ! the burden of the North
    Had pressed out all its lightness.
He gazed upon the unequal fight,
    His ranks all rent and gory,
And felt the shadow close like night
    Round his career of glory.

"General, come lead us!" loud the cry
    From a brave band was ringing—
"Lead us, and we will stop or die,
    That battery's awful singing."
He spurred to where his heroes stood,
    Twice wounded—no wound knowing—
The fire of battle in his blood
    And on his forehead glowing.

So Lyon died ! and well may flowers
    His place of burial cover,
For never had this land of ours
    A more devoted lover.
Living, his country was his bride,
    His life he gave her dying;
Life fortune, love—he naught denied
    To her and to her sighing.

Rest, Patriot, in thy hill-side grave,
    Beside her form who bore thee !
Long may the land thou diedst to serve
    Her bannered stars wave o'er thee !
Upon her history's brightest page,
    And on her Freedom's glowing portal,
She'll write thy grand, heroic rage,
    And grave thy name immortal ?

BATTLE ANTHEM.

BY JOHN NEIL.

Up, Christian warrior, up ! I hear
  The trumpet of the North
   . Sounding the charge !
  Fathers and sons, to horse !
  Fling the old standard forth,
   Blazing and large.

And now I hear the heavy tramp
  Of nations on the march,
   Silent as death !
  A slowly-gathering host,
  Like clouds o'er yonder arch,
   Holding their breath !

Our great blue sky is overcast ;
  And stars are dropping out,
   Through smoke and flame !
  Hail stones and coals of fire !
  Now comes the battle-shout !
   Jehovah's name !

And now the rebel pomp ! To prayer !
  Look to your stirrups, men !
   Yonder rides death !
  Now with a whirlwind sweep !
  Empty their saddles when
   Hot comes their breath !

As through the midnight forest tears
  With trumpeting and fire
   A thunder-blast ;
  So, Reapers, tear your way
Through yonder camp, until you hear,
" It is enough ! Put up thy sword !
  Oh, angel of the Lord !
   My wrath is past ! ''
       —*Portland (Me.) Transcript.*

THE CUMBERLAND.

BY H. W. LONGFELLOW.

At anchor in the Hampton Roads we lay,
  On board of the Cumberland sloop-of-war ;
And at times from the fortress across the bay
    The alarm of drums swept past,
    Or a bugle blast
  From the camp on shore.

Then far away to the south uprose
  A little feather of snow-white smoke,
And we knew that the iron ship of our foes
    Was steadily steering its course
    To try the force
  Of our ribs of oak.

Down upon us heavily runs,
  Silent and sullen, the floating fort ;
Then comes a puff of smoke from her guns ;
    And leaps the terrible death,
    With fiery breath,
  From each open port.

We are not idle, but send her straight
  Defiance back in a full broadside !
As hail rebounds from a roof of slate,
    Rebounds our heavier hail
    From each iron scale
  Of the monster's hide.

" Strike your flag ! " the rebel cries,
  In his arrogant. old plantation strain,
" Never ! " our gallant Morris replies ;
    " It is better to sink than to yield ! "
    And the whole air pealed
  With the cheers of our men.

Then, like a kraken, huge and black,
  She crushed our ribs in her iron grasp !

Down went the Cumberland all a wreck
  With a sudden shudder of death,
  And the cannon's breath
For her dying gasp.

Next morn, as the sun rose over the bay,
  Still floated our flag at the mainmast-head,
Lord, how beautiful was thy day !
  Every waft of air
  Was a whisper of prayer,
Or a dirge for the dead.

Ho ! brave hearts that went down in the sea,
  Ye are at peace in the troubled stream.
Ho ! brave land ! with hearts like these.
  Thy flag, that is rent in twain,
  Shall be one again,
And without a seam !

                           —*Atlantic Monthly.*

ROANOKE—Feb. 8, 1862.

[An Extract.]

BY GEORGE ALFRED TOWNSHEND.

Two awful days the foemen met,
  And when the third all glorious woke,
The spangled flag we worship yet,
  Curled all its stripes o'er Roanoke.

The corpse half buried in the sand,
  The far-off friends that wait the shock,
  The raven brooding on the rock,
The hungry sky, the lonesome band.

The blood, the tears, the sons, the sires—
  Oh! these too well the triumph note,
  Though ringing from the Nation's throat,
Acclaims that quench her funeral pyres.

We love and weep all unawares;
    The flag above, the dead beneath,
    The sabre dripping in its sheath,
And on our lips dear household prayers.

See mercy in the arms of fear,
    My God! this curse of blood revoke,
May every loyal Northern spear
    Be nerved with news from Roanoke.

THE CAPTURE OF FORT DONELSON.
February 16, 1862.

"McClernand's division, composed of Oglesby's, Wallace's and McArthur's brigades suffered terribly. They were composed of the Eighth, Ninth, Eleventh, Eighteenth, Twentieth, Twenty-ninth, Thirtieth, Thirty-first, Forty-fifth, Forty-eighth, and Forty-ninth Illinois regiments."

"The Eighth, Eighteenth, Twentieth and Thirty-first Illinois regiments occupied a position above the Fort."

"The four Illinois regiments held their ground full three hours. Nearly one third had been killed and wounded. Yet the balance stood firm."

O gales that dash th' Atlantic's swell
    Along our rocky shores!
Whose thunders diapason well
    New-England's glad hurrahs—

Bear to the prairies of the West
    The echoes of our joy,
The prayer that springs in every breast :
    "God bless thee—Illinois!"

Oh! awful hours, when grape and shell
    Tore through th' unflinching line;
"Stand firm, remove the men who fell,
    Close up and wait the sign."

It came at last, "Now lads the steel !"
    The rushing hosts deploy ;
"Charge, boys !"—the broken traitors reel—
    Huzza for Illinois!

In vain thy rampart, Donelson,
   The living torrent bars;
It leaps the wall, the fort is won,
   Up goes the Stripes and Stars.

Thy proudest mother's eyelids fill,
   As dares her gallant boy,
And Plymouth Rock and Bunker Hill
   Yearn to thee—Illinois.

Boston, February 22, 1862.

"OURS."

The following stanzas were written by Brig. Gen. Lander, on
hearing that the Confederate troops had said that "Fewer of
the Massachusetts officers would have been killed if they had
not been too proud to surrender."

We trust that the suggestion in the last stanza will be
promptly met, and the Twentieth Massachusetts be at once re-
cruited to its full complement.

Aye, deem us proud! for we are more
   Than proud of all our mighty dead;
Proud of the bleak and rock-bound shore
   A crowned oppressor cannot tread.

Proud of each rock, and wood, and glen,
   Of every river, lake, and plain;
Proud of the calm and earnest men
   Who claim the right and will to reign.

Proud of the men who gave us birth,
   Who battled with the stormy wave,
To sweep the red man from the earth,
   And build their homes upon his grave.

Proud of the holy summer morn,
   They traced in blood upon its sod;
The rights of freemen yet unborn,
   Proud of their language and their God.

Proud, that beneath our proudest dome,
　And round the cottage-cradled hearth,
There is a welcome and a home
　For every stricken race on earth.

Proud that yon slowly sinking sun
　Saw drowning lips grow white in prayer,
O'er such brief acts of duty done
　As honor gathers from despair.

Pride—'tis our watchword, " Clear the boats !"
　" Holmes, Putnam, Bartlett, Pierson—here !"
And while this crazy wherry floats,
　" Let's save our wounded !" cries Revere.

Old State—some souls are rudely sped—
　This record for thy Twentieth corps,
Imprisoned, wounded. dying, dead,
　It only asks, " Has Sparta more?"
                                    —*Boston Post.*

LANDER—March 8, 1862.

BY THOMAS BAILEY ALDRICH.

Close his bleak eyes—they shall no more
Flash victory where the cannon roar;
And lay the battered sabre at his side,
(His to the last, for so he would have died !)
Though he no more may pluck from out its sheath
The sinewy lightning that dealt traitors death.
Lead the worn war horse by the plumed bier—
Even his horse, now he is dead, is dear!

Take him, New England, now his work is done.
He fought the Good Fight valiantly—and won.
Speak of his daring. This man held his blood
Cheaper than water for the nation's good.
Rich Mountain, Fairfax, Romney—he was there.
Speak of him gently, of his mien, his air;

How true he was, how his strong heart could bend
With sorrow, like a woman's, for a friend;
Intolerant of every base desire;
Ice where he liked not; where he loved, all fire.

Take him, New England, gently.   Other days,
Peaceful and prosperous, shall give him praise.
How will our children's children breathe his name,
Bright on the shadowy muster-roll of fame !
Take him, New England, gently; you can fold
No purer patriot in your soft brown mould.

So, on New England's bosom, let him lie,
Sleeping awhile—as if the Good could die!

VOICE OF THE LOYAL NORTH.

BY OLIVER WENDELL HOLMES.

We sing "Our Country's" song to-night
    With saddened voice and eye;
Her banner droops in clouded light
    Beneath a wintry sky.
We'll pledge her once in golden wine
    Before her stars have set;
Though dim one reddened orb may shine,
    We have a country yet.

'Twas vain to sigh o'er errors past,
    The fault of sires or sons;
Our soldier heard the threatening blast
    And spiked his useless guns;
He saw the star-wreathed ensign fall
    By mad invaders torn;
But saw it from the bastioned wall
    That laughed their rage to scorn!

What though their angry cry is flung
    Across the howling wave—
They smite the air with idle tongue
    The gathering storm who brave;

Enough of speech! the trumpet rings;
  Be silent, patient, calm—
God help them if the tempest swings
  The pine against the palm!

Our toilsome years have made us tame;
  Our strength has slept unfelt;
The furnace fire is slow to flame
  That bids the ploughshares melt;
'Tis hard to lose the bread they win
  In spite of Nature's frowns,
To drop the iron threads we spin
  That weave our web of towns.

To see the rustling turbines stand
  Before the emptied flumes,
To fold the arms that flood the land
  With rivers from their looms—
But harder still for those who learn
  The truth forgot so long;
When once the slumbering passions burn,
  The peaceful are the strong!

The Lord have mercy on the weak,
  And calm the frenzied ire,
And save our brothers ere they shriek
  " We played with northern fire!"
The eagle holds his mountain height—
  The tiger pace his den!
Give all their country, each his right,
  God keep us all!   Amen!

———

HA! BOYS WHAT'S THAT WE HEAR?

BY OUR CORPORAL.

Ha! boys what's that we hear
Out of the South so clear?
Cannon and thunder cheer,
            True hearts and loyal!

Ay 'tis Du Pont at work,
Shellings the snakes that lurk
   Down by Port Royal!

Straight through Tennessee
The flag is flapping free—
   Ay, nothing shorter !
But first, with shot and shell,
The road was cleared right well—
Ye made each muzzle tell,
   Brave Foote and Porter.

Shear the old stripes and stars
Short, for the bloody bars?
   No, not an atom!
How, 'neath your cannon smoke,
Volley and charge and stroke,
Roar around Roanoke !
   Burnside is at 'em.

O brave lads of the West!
Joy to each valiant breast,
Three days of steady fight—
Three days of stormy night—
   Donelson tumbles.
Surrender out of hand !
" Unchivalrous demand!"
   (So Buckner grumbles).

March in, stout Grant and Smith,
(Ah! souls of pluck and pith),
Haul down for the old flag,
That black and bloody rag—
Twelve thousand in a bag!
   True hearts are overjoyed—
But half as many scamper,
(Ah ! there the only damper),
Through the very worst of weathers,
After old Fuss and Feathers
   And foul Barrabas Floyd.

ON THE SHORES OF TENNESSEE.

" Move my arm-chair, faithful Pompey;
    In the sunshine bright and strong,
For this world is fading, Pompey—
    Massa won't be with you long;
And I fain would hear the south wind
    Bring once more the sound to me,
Of the wavelets softly breaking
    On the shores of Tennessee.

" Mournful though the ripples murmur,
    As they still the story tell,
How no vessels float the banner
    That I've loved long and well.
I shall listen to their music,
    Dreaming that again I see
Stars and stripes on sloop and shallop
    Sailing up the Tennessee.

" And, Pompey, while old Massa's waiting
    For death's last dispatch to come,
If that exiled starry banner
    Should come proudly sailing home,
You shall greet it slave no longer—
    Voice and hand shall both be free
That shout and point to Union colors
    On the waves of Tennessee."

"Massa's berry kind to Pompey;
    But old darkey's happy here,
Where he's tended corn and cotton
    For dese many a long gone year.
Over yonder Missis's sleeping—
    No one tends her grave like me;
Mebbe she would miss the flowers
    She used to love in Tennessee.

" 'Pears like she was watching Massa—
    If Pompey should beside him stay,
Mebbe she'd remember better
    How for him she used to pray;

Telling him that way up yonder
  White as snow his soul would be,
If he served the Lord in Heaven
  While he lived in Tennessee."

Silently the tears were rolling
  Down the poor old dusky face,
As he stepped behind his master,
  In his long accustomed place.
Then a silence fell around them,
  As they gazed on rock and tree,
Pictured in the placid waters
  Of the rolling Tennessee.

Master, dreaming of the battle
  Where he fought by Marion's side,
When he bid the haughty Tarleton
  Stoop his lordly crest of pride.
Man, remembering how yon sleeper
  Once he held upon his knee,
E'er she loved the gallant soldier,
  Ralph Vervair, of Tennessee.

Still the south wind fondly lingers
  'Mid the veteran's silver hair;
Still the bondman close beside him
  Stands behind the old arm-chair.
With his dark-hued hand uplifted,
  Shading eyes, he bends to see
Where the woodland boldly jutting
  Turns aside the Tennessee.

Thus he watches cloud-born shadows
  Glide from tree to mountain-crest,
Softly creeping aye and ever
  To the river's yielding breast,
Ha! above the foliage yonder
  Something flutters wild and free!
"Massa! Massa! Hallelujah!
  The flag's come back to Tennessee!
  6

"Pompey, hold me on your shoulder,
    Help me stand on foot once more,
That I may salute the colors
    As they pass my cabin door.
Here's the paper signed that frees you,
    Give a freeman's shout with me—
'God and Union!' be our watchword
    Evermore in Tennessee!"

Then the trembling voice grew fainter,
    And the limbs refused to stand;
One prayer to Jesus—and the soldier
    Glided to that better land.
When the flag went down the river
    Man and master both were free;
While the ring-dove's note was mingled
    With the rippling Tennessee.
                              —*Harper's Weekly.*

THE WAY WE WENT TO BEAUFORT.

Full fifty sail we were that day,
When out to sea we sped away,
    With a feeling of brooding mystery ;
Bound—there was no telling where,
But well we knew there was strife to share,
And we felt our mission was bound to bear
    A place in heroic history.

The man at the helm, nothing knew he,
As he steered his ship out into the sea,
    On that morn of radiant beauty ;
And the ships outspread their wings. and flew
Like sea-birds over the water blue,
One thought alone each man of us knew—
    How best to do our duty.

Not a breath of wherefore or why was heard,
Not a doubting thought or a doubting word,

Or idle speculation ;
But a spirit of inspiring trust
Filled each man's breast, as it always must,
When leaders are brave, and a cause is just,
   And ours the cause of the nation.

And thus we went—the hurricane's breath
Was felt in our track, like the blast of death,
   But we had no thought of turning ;
Onward and onward the good fleet sped,
Locked in its breast the secret dread,
To break in gloom over treason's head,
   Where—we should soon be learning.

But brave Dupont and Sherman knew
Where the bolt should light, and each gallant crew
   Was ready to heed their orders.
Port Royal, Ho!—and a bright warm day,
We made the land many miles away,
And sullenly there before us lay
   Fierce Carolina's borders.

The mystery was all compassed then,
And the hearts of sea-sick, weary men,
   Cheered up, the prospect viewing ;
There is that grit in the human mind,
However gentle, or good, or kind,
That is always to double its fist inclined,
   When near where a fight is brewing.

The rebel guns waked a fearful note
From our rifled cannon's open throat,
   And our shells flew fast and steady.
The battle is over—the strife is done—
The Stars and Bars from the forts have run—
The blow is struck, and victory won—
   Beaufort is ours already.

"WITH THY SHIELD, OR UPON IT."

BY S. C. MERCER.

The loss of a shield was regarded as peculiarly disgraceful
by the Greek soldiers. The dead were borne home upon their
shields. "Return with thy shield, my son, or upon it," was
the heroic injunction of a Spartan mother.

Sound the trumpet, sound ! The die is cast,
The Rubicon of fate is passed,
The loyal and the rebel hosts,
Kentucky, throng thy leaguered coasts,
And on the issue of the strife
Hang peace and liberty and life ;
All that the storied past endears,
And all the hopes of coming years ;
The startled world looks on the field—
Thou canst not fly—thou dar'st not yield—
Then strike ! and make thy foemen feel
Thy triply-consecrated steel,   .
And *with* or *on* thy shining shield,
Return, Kentucky, from the field.

Strike ! though the battle's dead be strown
O'er land and wave, from zone to zone ;
Strike ! though the gulf of human blood
Roll o'er thee like the primal flood.
Treason at home—beyond the sea
Its ally, ancient tyranny,
Democracy's relentless foe,
Aim at thy heart their deadliest blow ;
Freedom's last hope remains with thee,
O armies of democracy !
Then lead thy martial hosts abroad
In the grand panoply of God,
And *with* or *on* thy shining shield
Return, Kentucky, from the field.

Wave, banners, wave, and let the sky
Glow with your flashing wings on high,

There's music in each rustling fold
Sweeter than minstrel ever told.
Oh ! who that ever heard the story
Of all our dead who fell in glory,
Still pressing where the starry light
Streamed like a meteor o'er the fight,
Till their expiring bosoms poured
The red libation of the sword,
Would leave Kentucky *now*, or thrust
Her beaming forehead in the dust,
Where treason's reptiles writhe and hiss
Like fiends shut out from Eden's bliss ?
Better the freeman's lowliest grave
Than golden fetters of a slave ;
Then *with* or *on* thy shining shield
Return, Kentucky, from the field.

If bribed by lust of power or gold,
Thy country's welfare thou hast sold,
Iscariot-like thy name shall be
In Freedom's dark Gethsemane ;
Disgrace and fell remorse shall plow
Eternal furrows o'er thy brow ;
By angels, men, and fiends abhorred—
Like Judas who betrayed his Lord.
Outcast at home—across the sea,
Shunned like a leper thou shalt be—
No spring shall slake thy burning thirst,
The fire shall shun thee as accursed—
Day shall be cheerless—no repose
At night thy swollen eye shall close—
Lift to indignant Heaven thine eye,
Curse God in black despair and die !
Kentucky, hast thou son so base
Thy fame unsullied would disgrace?
Attaint his blood, disown his race,
His line, his very name efface.

Then charge ! thy grand battalions free
From all attaint of treachery—
Charge on thy foes ! make all the air
Vocal with Freedom's holiest prayer,
And *with* or *on* thy shining shield,
Return, Kentucky, from the field !

State of the " Dark and Bloody Ground,"
The trumpet peals its final sound,
Down every mountain height, arrayed,
Comes thundering on the long brigade ;
By every valley, pass. and river,
Sabres and bayonets flash and quiver ;
Shame to the faithless son who falters
When impious hands assail their altars,
And fill each font of happiness
With waves of woe and bitterness ;
The dead their august shades present
By Frankfort's battle monument—
Not now their souls can be at rest,
Though in the Islands of the Blest—
" Remember us, " their voices cry,
" When comes the hour of conflict nigh.
Draw on the traitor ranks abhorred
The sword of Gideon and the Lord !
And *with* or *on* thy shining shield,
Return, Kentucky, from the field ! "

GRANDPA NATHAN.

[Respectfully inscribed to Gen. Leslie Coombs.]

BY WILLIAM D. GALLAGHER.

By the beech and hickory fire
　Grandpa Nathan sat at night,
With details of marching armies,
　And the news of many a fight,
When he laid aside the paper,
　Though its contents he had told,

He was plied with many questions
  By the young and by the old.
It's a war the most infernal,
  (Grandpa Nathan made reply),
But the legions of the Union
  Soon will crush it out, or die !
If I only had the vigor
  Of just twenty years ago,
How I'd leap into my saddle !
  How I'd fly to meet the foe !

Nannie Hardin, dearest daughter,
  There's a spirit now abroad
That's akin to whatsoever
  Is at enmity with God.
It has wrought upon a portion
  Of the people of the land,
Till they almost think they're honest
  In the treason they have plann'd.
It has struck the sea with rapine,
  It has tinged its shores with blood,
And it rolls and surges inland
  Like a desolating flood.
It has rent the nearest kindred—
  E'en the mother and the son;
But, as God's a God of Justice,
  Its career will soon be run.

There's a camp in Wickliffe's meadow,
  Less than eighteen miles away—
John at your age I could make it
  Twice 'twixt now and break of day;
Fill your buggy up with baskets,
  Fill each basket to the brim,
Sweep the pantry of its choicest,
  Till the shelves are lean and slim;
Take a jug or two of apple,
  For these chill November damps

Oft benumb the weary sentries
  As they guard the sleeping camps.
Drive the pet of old Sarpedon—
  For the glory of his sires
He will make the camp at Wickliffe
  Ere they stir the morning fires.

Tell the soldier of Kentucky,
  And the soldier from abroad
Who has come to fight the battle
  Of his country and his God—
Tell them one who on the Wabash
  Fought with Daviess when he fell,
And who bled at Meigs, where Dudley
  Met the painted hosts of hell—
One who fought with Hart at Raisin,
  And with Johnson on the Thames,
And with Jackson at New Orleans,
  Where we won immortal names,
Sends them from his chimney corner
  Such fair greeting as he may,
With a few small creature-comforts
  For this drear November day.

Tell them he has watched this quarrel
  From its outbreak until now,
And, with hand upon his heart-beat,
  And God's light upon his brow,
He invokes their truest manhood,
  The full prowess of their youth,
In this battle of the Nation
  For the right and for the truth.
Tell them one whose years are sinking
  To the quiet of the grave,
Thus enjoins each valiant spirit
  That would scorn to be a slave—
" By the toil and blood your fathers
  In the cause of Freedom spent,
By the memory of your mothers,
  And the noble aid they lent—

By the blessings God has showered
  On this birthright of the free,
Give to Heaven a reverent spirit,
  Bend to Heaven a willing knee,
And in silence, 'mid the pauses
  Of the hymn and of the prayer,
To the God of Hosts appealing,
  By the God of Battles swear—
Swear to rally round the standard
  With our nation that was born,
With its Stars of world-wide glory,
  And its Stripes that none may scorn!
Swear to fight the fight forced on us,
  While an armed foe stirs abroad;
Swear to fight the fight of Freedom,
  Of the Union, and of God!"

Ah! he drives the young Sarpedon—
  Drives the son of glorious sires,
And he'll make the camp at Wickliffe's
  Ere they build the morning fires.
Do you know, child, I am prouder
  Of the spirit of your boy,
Than of any other grandson
  That e'er brought his mother joy?
And so now, good Nannie Hardin,
  For the night you'd best retire;
As for me, my child, I'm wakeful,
  And I'll still sit by the fire.
Oh, my soul is in the battles
  Of the Wabash and the Thames,
Where the prowess of Kentucky
  Won imperishable names!

I must see the camp at Wickliffe's,
  Nannie, you as well can go;
I must mingle with the soldiers .
  Who have come to meet our foe;

I must talk to them of battles
  By the ranks of Freedom won,
And of acts of valor ventured,
  And of deeds of daring done.
Ah, I'll take them to the ramparts
  Where their fathers fought of old,—
For my spirit now surveys them,
  As a chart that is unrolled,—
And I'll show them in the mirror
  Of the clouds and of the skies,
Where the hosts of glory marshal,
  And the flag of glory flies.

Take a blanket, dear, from Effie,
  And a comfort here and there,
And from my good bed and wardrobe
  Strip whatever I can spare.
Hunt the house from top to bottom,
  And let the neighbors know
What they need, the men who shield them
  From the fury of the foe.
Be up early in the morning;
  Ask of all what they will send
To the camp in Wickliffe's meadow,
  Where each soldier is a friend.
'Twere a sin, whilst there is plenty,
  (Let *us* never feel the taunt,)
That the legions of the Union,
  Braving danger, were in want.

Write at once to Hatty Shelby,
  And—for both of them are there—
Send a line to Alice Dudley,
  And a word for Ruth Adair;
Then to-morrow write to Dorcas,
  And anon to Mollie Todd,—
Say they've work now for their country,
  For their freedom, and their God;

And if only half the spirit
  That their mother had is theirs,
There'll be rapid work with needles,
  And sharp rummaging up stairs.
Oh, it stirs the blood of seventy,
  Wherever it survives,
Just to touch the chain of memory
  Of the old Kentucky wives !

In a day or two—at farthest
  When the present rain is done—
You and I will take the carriage.
  With the rising of the sun,
And we'll spend a day or longer,
  With the soldiers in their camps,
Taking stores that best may shield them
  From the chill November damps.
Oh, I'll cheer them on to battle—
  And I'll stir each lofty soul,
As I paint the fields of honor
  Where the drums of glory roll!
And I'll bid them never falter,
  While there's treason still abroad,
In this battle of the Nation,
  For our Union, and for God.

One who fought upon the Wabash
  By Joe Daviess when he fell,
And who bled at Meigs with Dudley,
  When we met the hosts of hell;
One who fought with Hart at Raisin,
  And with Johnson on the Thames,
And with Jackson at New Orleans.
  Where we won immortal names,
Will be listened to with patience
  By the heroes now at hand,   ·
Who have rushed on to our rescue,
  In this peril of the land.

By the memory of our fathers,
  By the brave, and by the just,
This rebellion shall be vanquished.
  Though each traitor bite the dust.

NEW ORLEANS WON BACK.

BY ROBERT LOWELL.

God made the youths to walk unscathed
  In the furnace seven times hot;
And when smoky flames our squadron bathed,
  Amid horrors of shell and shot,
Then, too, it was God that brought them through
  That death-crowded thoroughfare,
So now at six bells the church pennons flew,
  And the crews went all to prayer.
Thank God! thank God! our men won the fight,
  Against forts, and fleet, and flame;
Thank God! they have given our flag its right
  In a town that brought it shame.
      Oh, up in the morning, up in the morning,
        Upon in the morning early!
      Our flag hung there in the bright still air,
        With smoke flowing soft and curly.

Ten days for the deep ships at the bar;
  Six days for the mortar fleet,
That battered the great forts from afar;
  And then, to that deadly street!
A flash!   Our strong ships snapped the boom,
  To the fire-rafts and the forts,
To crush and crash, and flash and gloom,
  And iron beaks fumbling their ports.
From the dark came the raft, in flame and smoke;
  In the dark came the iron beak;
But our sailor's hearts were stouter than oak,
  And the false foe's iron weak.

Oh, up in the morning, up in the morning,
  Up in the morning early!
Before they knew, they had burst safe through,
  And left the forts, grim and burly.

Though it be brute's work, not man's, to tear
  Live limbs like shivered wood;
Yet, to dare, and to stand, and to take death for
   share,
  Are as much as the angels could.
Our men towed the blazing rafts ashore;
  They battered the great rams down;
Scarce a wreck floated where was a fleet before,
  When our ships came up to the town.
There were miles of batteries yet to be dared,
  But they quenched these all, as in play;
Then, with their yards squared, their guns' mouths
   bared,
  They held the great town at bay.
     Oh, up in the morning, up in the morning,
      Up in the morning early!
      Our stout ships came through shell, shot and
       flame,
      But the town will not always be surly.

For this Crescent City takes to its breast
  The Father of Waters' tide;
And here shall the wealth of our world, in the West,
  Meet wealth of the world beside;
Here the date palm and the olive find
  A near and equal sun;
And a hundred broad, deep rivers wind
  To a summer sea in one;
Here the Fall steals all old winter's ice,
  And the spring steals all his snow;
While he but smiles at their artifice,
  And like his own nature go.
     Oh, up in the morning, up in the morning,
      Up in the morning early!

May that flag float here till the earth's last
    year,
With the lake mists, fair and pearly.
                  —*N. Y. Evening Post.*

THE VARUNA—April 25th, 1862.

BY GEORGE H. BOKER.

Who has not heard of the dauntless Varuna?
    Who has not heard of the deeds she has done?
Who shall not hear, while the brown Mississippi
    Rushes along from the snow to the sun?

Crippled and leaking she entered the battle,
    Sinking and burning she fought through the fray,
Crushed were her sides and the waves ran across
    her,
    Ere, like a death-wounded lion at bay,
Sternly she closed in the last fatal grapple,
    Then in her triumph moved grandly away.

Five of the rebels, like satellites round her,
    Burned in her orbit of splendor and fear;
One, like the Pleiad of mystical story,
    Shot, terror-stricken, beyond her dread sphere.

We who are waiting with crowns for the victors,
    Though we should offer the wealth of our store,
Load the Varuna from deck down to kelson,
    Still would be niggard, such tribute to pour
On courage so boundless. It beggars possession,
    It knocks for just payment at heaven's bright door!

Cherish the heroes who fought the Varuna ;
    Treat them as kings if they honor your way;
Succor and comfort the sick and the wounded;
    Oh! for the dead, let us all kneel to pray.

JUNE 4th, 1862.

The President calls for 300,000 volunteers for the
war.

"KISS ME, MOTHER, AND LET ME GO!"

BY MISS PRIEST.

Have you heard the news that I heard to-day?
 The news that trembles on every lip?
The sky is darker again, they say,
 And the breakers threaten the good old ship.
Our country calls on her sons again,
 To strike, in her name, at a dastard foe;
She asks for six hundred thousand men,
 I would be one, mother. Let me go.

The love of country was born with me;
 I remember how my young heart would thrill
When I used to sit on my grandame's knee
 And list to the story of Bunker Hill.
Life gushed out there in a rich red blood;
 My grandsire fell in that fight, you know;—
Would you have me shame the brave old blood?
 Nay, kiss me, mother, and let me go.

Our flag, the flag of our hope and pride,
 With its stars and stripes and its field of blue,
Is mocked, insulted, torn down, defied,
 And trampled upon by the rebel crew,
And England and France look on and sneer,
 "Ha, queen of the earth, thou art fallen low,"
Earth's down trodden millions weep and fear,
 So kiss me, mother, and let me go.

Under the southern burning skies,
 Our brothers languish in heartsick pain,
They turn to us with their pleading eyes;
 Oh, mother, say, shall they turn in vain?
Their ranks are thinning from sun to sun,
 Yet bravely they hold at bay the foe,
Shall we let them die there, one by one?
 Nay, kiss me, mother, and let me go.

Can you selfishly cling to your household joys,
    Refusing the smallest tithe to yield,
While thousands of mothers are sending boys
    Beloved as yours to the battle field?
Can you see my country call in vain,
    And restrain my arm from the needful blow?
Not so; though your heart should break with pain,
    You will kiss me, mother, and let me go.

"KISS ME, MOTHER, AND LET ME GO!"

A MOTHER'S REPLY.

BY M. C. M.

I have heard the news which came that day,
    I have read it all with a trembling lip;
I know that dangers surround our way
    And perils threaten the good old ship.
I have heard the summons to loyal men,
    The call for six hundred thousand more,
The call which has sounded again and again,
    Louder, more urgent than ever before.

Your message too, my own brave son,
    I have read it o'er and o'er,
And you were dearer to me, when done,
    Than ever you were before,
How proud I felt of my noble boy;
    Yet sadly the tears would flow,
When I read with a grief that was almost joy,
    " Kiss me, mother, and let me go."

It seems but a moment, since on my breast
    I cradled my first born son,
Since in these arms you were hushed to rest;
    How quickly the years have gone !
How well I remember when you were a child,
    Who shouted, and laughed, and ran;
It seems like a dream, or a fancy wild,
    That my little boy now is a man.

But now, in the hour of my country's need,
  Assailed by a deadly foe,
Can I hold you back? 'twere a traitor's deed,
  My darling, I bid you go.
Go forth in the cause of your native land,
  My heart shall not fail at the sight,
Let the thought of your mother but nerve your hand
  In the struggle for freedom and right.

I shall think of you often, my own brave son,
  When thousand of miles away;
I will pray for you always, my precious one,
  As mothers alone can pray.
And if on the battle-field, far from my side,
  The head that I love shall lie low,
I will say, It is well: for his country he died;
  God bless you, my darling one: Go.

Brookfield, Aug. 19.

TO CANAAN!

A SONG OF THE SIX HUNDRED THOUSAND.

Where are you going, soldiers,
  With banner, gun and sword?
We're marching South to Canaan
  To battle for the Lord!
What Captain leads your armies
  Along the rebel coasts?
The Mighty One of Israel,
  His name is Lord of Hosts!

      To Canaan, to Canaan
      The Lord has led us forth,
      To blow before the heathen walls
      The trumpets of the North!

What flag is this you carry,
  Along the sea and shore?
The same our grandsires lifted up,—
  The same our fathers bore!

In many a battle's tempest
It shed the crimson rain,—
What God has woven in his loom
Let no man rend in twain!

> To Canaan, to Canaan
> The Lord has sent us forth,
> To plant upon the rebel towers
> The banners of the North!

What troop is this that follows,
All armed with picks and spades?
These are swarthy bondsmen,—
The iron-skinned brigades!
They'll pile up Freedom's breastwork,
They'll scoop out rebels' graves;
Who then will be their owner
And march them off for slaves?

> To Canaan, to Canaan,
> The Lord has led us forth,
> To strike upon the captive's chain
> The hammers of the North!

What song is this you're singing?
The same that Israel sung
When Moses led the mighty choir,
And Miriam's timbrel rung!
To Canaan! To Canaan!
The priests and maidens cried;
To Canaan! To Canaan!
The people's voice replied.

> To Canaan, to Canaan
> The Lord has led us forth,
> To thunder through its adder dens,
> The anthems of the North!

When Canaan's hosts are scattered,
And all her walls are flat,
What follows next in order?
—— The Lord will see to that!

We'll break the tyrant's sceptre,—
We'll build the people's throne,—
When half the world is Freedom's,
Then all the world's our own!

To Canaan, to Canaan,
The Lord has led us forth,
To sweep the rebel threshing floors,
A whirlwind from the North!

The thrilling, Cromwellian sort of war song, "To Canaan," which we copy above from the *Transcript*, was sung at a war meeting in Salem, set to appropriate music by Gen H. K. Oliver.

BABES IN THE WOOD.

BY C. C.

So you've buried the flag at Memphis ?
How many fathoms deep ?
What seal did you set on the Stars and Stripes?
And who that grave shall keep?

Alas, for the dead at Memphis!
Mere dust to dust you bear;
No vision of Life all glorified,
Of Love grown heavenly fair;—

No radiant dream, with a Christly sign,
Of the victor's living palm;
Of the odorous golden joy that dares
Join seraphs in their psalm!

You never read, in a rich man's cave
The Life of a world lay, slain!
And the mourning women went to watch,
But found—where he *had* lain.

Come, guess—Who roll'd from his cave the rock ?
Who broke great Pilate's seal?—
While the soldiers sleep, and the women weep,
Base hands the Body steal.

Vain guess for knowledge ! Children dear,
    Not Death lay in that cave,
But Living Love ! While the world above
    Went wailing, '' *Died to save !* ''

Well—judge if Freedom's sacred sign
    Can moulder under ground,
With the march of a million men o'erhead,
    Their banners eagle-crowned?

From Plymouth Rock to the Golden Gate,
    A shout goes right and left;
The alien's dreamful watch is done—
    The sepulchre is cleft.

Weak hands ! Heap clay on the stars of God !
    They never shone before !
They rend the shroud, and they pierce the cloud;
    All hail, then, Thirty-Four !
              —*The Independent.*

THE ENSIGN OF WARWICK.

BY G. N. BRIGHAM.

The smoke of battle settled from the field
    Where Warwick checked our firm, advancing line;
And with Vermont's proud boys there lay a shield,
    The Stars and Stripes, the Stag's Head and the
        Pine.

And where was seen the reck and wreck of all
    That strife, the bearer of his Country's Sign
Lay bleeding ! Stoutly had he led the call,
    And stalwart, stood waving his Mountain Pine.

But in that fire-hurled hail, when thundered loud
    The rifle-pits that fronted all our line,
His stalwart form went down, as when a cloud
    Quick flashes, and the lightning scathes some pine.

"Comrade," said he, " I have a wound: to you
  I trust a message.   Put your hand in mine.
I have a mother; tell her I was true
  To our Old Flag, Vermont, her Star and Pine.

" A sister, too,I have at home—a sweet,
  Good child. She plants for me the myrtle vine;
But tell her, soldier, that we shall not meet:
  I led at Warwick with the Stars and Pine!

" A brother—his a heart with kindness stored—
  Follows the plow and yards the milking kine;
He hardly ever took my father's sword
  And belt, or plumed his cap with sprig of pine.

"Tell him our Flag displays the sheaf of grain,
  Nor rebel hand hath plucked it yet from mine;
That, as a soldier, I have left no stain—
  Have served my country well—the Stars and Pine.

" And, comrade, to another say, farewell!
  (A wife's fond love, perhaps, is luck of thine,)
For her I fear, I fear—to have you tell
  How that I fell, bearing the Stars and Pine.

" But break it to her tenderly, and say
  The foe was dealt with sore—our charge was fine;
And tell her I was proud to bear that day
  The Union Flag, the Stag's Head and the Pine !'

" Comrade, to me the sun shall bring no morn;
  The bugle's call disturb no ear of mine:
But on! ay on! the foe shall never scorn
  The Lincoln Flag of Stars, Vermont's green
    Pine. "

———

AUGUST 8th, 1862,

The President calls for 300,000 more Volunteers.

THE DRAFTED WIDE-AWAKE.

I was a glorious Wide-Awake,
  All marching in a row;
And wore a shiny oil-cloth cape,
  About two years ago.
Our torches flared with turpentine,
  And filled the street with smoke;
And we were sure whate'er might come,
  Secession was a joke.
        Oh, if I then had only dreamed
          The things that now I know,
        I ne'er had been a Wide-Awake
          About two years ago.

I said the South would never dare
  To strike a single blow;
I thought that they were cowards then,
  About two years ago.
And so I marched behind a rail,
  Armed with a wedge and maul;
With Honest Abe upon a flag,
  A boatman gaunt and tall.
        Oh if I then had only dreamed
          The things which now I know,
        I ne'er had been a Wide-Awake
          About two years ago.

My work was good, my wages high,
  And bread and coal was low,
The silver jingled in my purse
  About two years ago.
In peace my wife and chi'dren dwelt,
  Happy the live long day;
And war was but the fearful curse
  Of countries far away.
        Oh, if I then had only dreamed
          The things which now I know,
        I ne'er had been a Wide-Awake
          About two years ago.

My wife sits pale and weeping now,
  My children crying low;
I did not think to go to war
  About two years ago.
And no one now will earn their food,
  No one will be their shield;
God help them when I lie in death
  Upon the bloody field.
        Oh, if I then had only dreamed
          The things which now I know,
        I ne'er had been a Wide-Awake
        About two years ago.

One brother's bones half buried lie
  Near the Antietam's flow;
He was a merry, happy lad
  About two years ago.
And where the Chickahominy
  Moves sluggish towards the sea,
Was left another's wasted corpse—
  I am the last of three.
        Oh, if I then had only dreamed
          The things which now I know,
        I ne'er had been a Wide-Awake
        About two years ago.

Just now I saw my torch and cape,
  Which once made such a show;
They are not now what they seemed
  About two years ago.
I thought I carried freedom's light,
  In that smoky, flamy band;
I've learned I bore destruction's torch—
  That wedge has split the land.
        Oh, if I then had only dreamed
          The things which now I know,
        I ne'er had been a Wide-Awake
        About two years ago.

THE COWARDS ARE COMING.

The cowards are coming, O dear, O dear!
The cowards are coming, O dear, O dear!
    With fugitive speed,
    They are coming indeed,
And their faces are pallid with fear.
This wretched skedaddle (I name it with pain),
Commenced in loyal, lumbering Maine :
With instinctive cunning and recreant craft.
They clear'd at the 'smell' of the purgative 'draught.'
    The cowards are coming, &c.

They are flying like sheep in a state of dismay,
When the wolves are out prowling in search of their
    prey;
    They are running pell-mell
    Over mountain and dell,
So fast that they are skulking away, away.
They are scampering off thro' mire and mud,
The roll of the drum makes the renegades scud;
O'er the Boundary Line they're scudding in swarms,
Deserting e'en their "companions in arms."
    The cowards are coming, &c.

Though the exile from bondage we hail with a smile,
And he's free as air on Canadian soil;
    Yet we know how to treat
    Every runaway cheat,
That shrinks from the patriot's toil, his toil,
We will do what we can this vile stampede to stem,
We shall have a " fugitive slave law " for them,
And back into service we'll render the knaves,
They're the meanest and vilest of " fugitive slaves."
    The cowards are coming, O dear, O dear,
    The cowards are coming, O dear, O dear,
    With fugitive speed.
    They are coming indeed,
And their faces are pallid with fear, with fear.
        —*Canadian Press.*

HEROES.

BY EDNA DEAN PROCTOR.

Mother Earth! are the Heroes dead?
Do they thrill the heart of the years no more?
Are the gleaming snows and the poppies red
All that is left of the brave of yore?
Are there none to fight as Theseus fought,
Far in the young world's misty dawn?
Or to teach as the mild-eyed Nestor taught—
Mother Earth! are the Heroes gone?

Gone? In a grander form they rise—
Dead? We can clasp their hands in ours—
And light our path by their shining eyes,
And wreathe their brows with immortal flowers,
Wherever a noble deed is done,
'Tis the pulse of a Hero's heart is stirred;
Wherever right has a triumph won,
There are the Heroes' voices heard.

Their armor rings on a nobler field
Than the Greek and the Trojan fiercely trod,
For Freedom's sword is the blade they wield,
And the light above is the smile of God.
So, in his isle of calm delight,
Jason may sleep the years away,
For *the Heroes live* and the sky is bright,
And the world is a braver world to-day.

K. T. DID.

We learn from Kansas Territory that Captain Jennison, of border fame, has offered six hundred of his well-known "Jay-Hawkers," all bold riders and well mounted, to the Union cause; also, that other mounted regiments will shortly be organized. Good for K. T — *Western Paper.*

From her borders far away
　　Kansas blows a trumpet call,
Answered by the loud " hurrah ! "
　　Of her troopers, one and all.

8

"Knife and pistol, sword and spur!"
        Cries K. T.
"Let my troopers all concur
To the old flag, no demur,
        Follow me!"

Hence the song of jubilee,
Platyphillis from the tree,
High among the branches hid,
Sings all night so merrily—
        "K. T. did,
        She did—she did!"

Thirty score Jay-Hawkers bold,
    Kansas men of strong renown,
Rally round the banner old,
    Casting each his gauntlet down.
"Good for Kansas," one and all
        Cry to hear;
Riding to her trumpet call,
Blithe as to a festival,
        All concur!

Hence the revel and the glee,
As the chanter from the tree,
High among the branches hid,
Sings all night so merrily—
        "K. T. did!
        She did—she did!"
                —*Vanity Fair.*

RALLYING SONG.

BY MRS. L. S. GOODWIN.

Rally, men and brothers, rally!
    'Tis the time for you and me;
We will stand by one another
    Round the standard of the free.

Hark ! we hear our gallant brothers
  Who are battling with the foe,
Calling—" Come, Oh! come and help us !"
  Is the answer YES—or No ?

Now OR NEVER ! is the watchword—
  When our locks are turned to gray,
That we fought, or that we faltered,
  Which shall be the story—Say ?

Like the prairie flowers for number,
  Western soldiers rise and go,—
Shall New England lack her quotas ?
  God and Massachusetts, No!

Where would be the homes we cling to
  Could Rebellion gain the day ?
All together we WILL crush him,
  Grind the monster vile to clay.

Leave the desk, and leave the counter,
  Farm and workshop—no delay;
Rush ! our glorious UNION needs us,
  Not to-morrow, but TO-DAY !
Boston, August 13, 1862.

———

TO THE NINTH VERMONT REGIMENT.

BY C. R. BALLARD.

Full many a brave Vermonter
  Is in the field to-day,
Among the foremost, waiting
  Impatient for the fray.
But while there yet is needed
  Courage without alloy,
How fitting sounds the summons—
  " *Come on, Green-Mountain Boy !*"

From many a quiet village,
  From hillside, vale and glen;
From homes, whose faithful teachings
  Make earnest, living men,
There comes a band of heroes,
  Of firm and fearless front;
Destined to deeds of valor—
  The gallant Ninth Vermont.

Heed, then, your Country's Summons,
  When hearts as stout and brave
As ever beat with longings
  A Nation's life to save.
Down where opposing armies
  Are marshaled for the fight,
Make haste to do fierce battle
  For Liberty and Right.

Down where Potomac's waters ·
  Are red with brother's blood;
Nay, where the brave Vermonters
  Faced murderous fire and flood;
Prove that the self same spirit
  Your every bosom thrills,
That fired that band of martyrs—
  The heroes of Lee's Mills.

Show by your gallant bearing
  The Mountains whence you came;
Amid the thickening contest
  Call Ethan Allen's name.
And then with shout terrific
  As cannon's stunning noise,
Sustain the reputation
  Of "The brave Green-Mountain Boys!"

———

  "We are living, we are dwelling
    In a grand and awful time;
  In an age on ages telling:
    To be living is sublime."

THREE HUNDRED THOUSAND MORE.

We are coming, Father Abraham—three hundred
thousand more,
From Mississippi's winding stream and from New
England's shore:
We leave our plows and work-shops, our wives and
children dear,
With hearts too full for utterance, with but a silent
tear;
We dare not look behind us, but steadfastly before—
We are coming, Father Abraham—three hundred
thousand more!

If you look across the hill-tops that meet the northern sky,
Long moving lines of rising dust your vision may
descry;
And now the wind, an instant, tears the cloudy veil
aside,
And floats aloft our spangled flag in glory and in
pride;
And bayonets in the sunlight gleam, and bands brave
music pour—
We are coming, Father Abraham—three hundred
thousand more!

If you look all up our valleys, where the growing
harvests shine,
You may see our sturdy farmer-boys fast forming
into line;
And children from their mother's knees are pulling
at the weeds,
And learning how to reap and sow, against their
country's needs;
And a farewell group stands weeping at every cot-
tage door.
We are coming, Father Abraham—three hundred
thousand more!

You have called us, and we're coming, by Richmond's
　　bloody tide,
To lay us down for freedom's sake our brothers'
　　bones beside;
Or from foul treason's savage grasp to wrench the
　　murderous blade,
And in the face of foreign foes its fragments to pa-
　　rade.
Six hundred thousand loyal men and true have gone
　　before.
We are coming, Father Abraham—three hundred
　　thousand more!

　　　　　　　　　　　　—*N. Y. Evening Post.*

　　　　　　　　　　WHY!

BY RICHARD STORRS LEWIS.

Twenty millions held at bay !
　Why, Northmen, why?
Less than half maintain the day !
　Why, Northmen, why?
With the sturdy iron will, the skill,
With the blood of Bunker Hill—
　Why, Northmen, why?

Standing yet are Sumter's walls—
　Why, Northmen, why?
Slumbering yet th' avenging balls !
　Why, Northmen, why?
Charleston left to scoff at ease !
Richmond vaunting as it please!
Traitor taunts on every breeze !—
　Why, Northmen, why?

Hear our wounded eagle wail !
　Why, Statesmen. why?
See our spangled banner trail !
　Why, Statesmen, why?

Coward England mocks amain!
Courtly Paris shrugs disdain!
Cordial Russia throbs with pain!--
  Why, Statesmen, why?

By this fierce but fruitless fight,
  On! Leaders, on!
By your waste of loyal might,
  On! Leaders, on!
By the blood that soaks the sod,
By the brave that bite the clod,
By the souls gone up to God!--
  On! Leaders, on!

By our past, so bright-renown'd,
  On! Northmen, on!
By the South, deceived, misled,
By our hundred thousand dead,
Who for South and North have bled!--
  On! Northmen, on!
                    —*Once a Month.*

THE BATTLE AUTUMN OF 1862.

The flags of war like storm-birds fly,
  The charging trumpets blow;
Yet rolls no thunder in the sky,
  No earthquake strives below.

And, calm and patient, Nature keeps
  Her ancient promise well,
Though o'er her bloom and greenness sweeps
  The battle's breath of hell.

And still she walks in golden hours
  Through harvest-happy farms,
And still she wears her fruits and flowers
  Like jewels on her arms.

What mean the gladness of the plain,
  This joy of eve and morn,

The mirth that shakes the beard of grain
   And yellow locks of corn?
Ah! eyes may well be full of tears,
   And hearts with hate are hot;
But even-paced come round the years,
   And nature changes not.

She meets with smiles our bitter grief,
   With songs our groans of pain;
She mocks with tint of flower and leaf
   The war-field's crimson stain.

Still, in the cannon's pause, we hear
   Her sweet thanksgiving-psalm;
Too near to God for doubt or fear,
   She shares the eternal calm.

She knows the seed lies safe below
   The fires that blast and burn;
For all the tears of blood we sow
   She waits the rich return.

She sees with clearer eye than ours
   The good of suffering born,—
The hearts that blossom like her flowers
   And ripen like our corn.

Oh, give to us, in times like these,
   The vision of her eyes;
And make her fields and fruited trees
   Our golden prophecies!

Oh, give to us her finer ear!
   Above this stormy din,
We, too, would hear the bells of cheer
   Ring peace and freedom in!
                  —*Atlantic Monthly.*

Contents of Part I.

Part II will be published soon, and will contain the remainder of the most popular Songs of the War.

www.ingramcontent.com/pod-product-compliance
Lightning Source LLC
Chambersburg PA
CBHW030552270326
41927CB00008B/1614